the power of stillness

the power of stillness

learn
meditation
in 30 days

Tobin Blake

NEW WORLD LIBRARY
NOVATO, CALIFORNIA

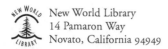 New World Library
14 Pamaron Way
Novato, California 94949

Front cover design by Mary Ann Casler
Text design and typography by Tona Pearce Myers

The material in this book is intended for education. It is not meant to take the place of diagnosis and treatment by a qualified medical practitioner or therapist. No expressed or implied guarantee as to the effects of the use of the recommendations can be given nor liability taken.

Library of Congress Cataloging-in-Publication Data
Blake, Tobin
  The power of stillness : learning meditation in 30 days / by Tobin Blake.
       p.   cm.
Includes bibliographical references.
ISBN 1-57731-242-2 (pbk. : alk. paper)
1. Meditation. I. Title.
BL627 .B54 2003
158.1'2—dc21   2002154751

First Printing, April 2003
ISBN 978-1-57731-242-2

10 9 8 7

For Lourdes,
fine company along a fine way

contents

part 1

mapping the road ahead   1

part 2

the journey begins   35
a thirty-day workbook

part 3

the journey continues   185

acknowledgments

n o book is written and produced by the author alone. In my life, I have been blessed, and sometimes I think cursed, by the company of extraordinary people in this extraordinary time. Each of my friends and family has contributed something to this book, by contributing something to who I am today. So first of all, my thanks go out to them. Without their influence in my life, this book would never have been written. Here, though, I can only name a few who have given directly of their time, spirit, and energy to make this book shine — or even possible at all:

Susan Crawford, of the Crawford Literary Agency, for handling the business end of this project.

Dr. John Dresser, of the Oregon Research Institute, for his help with some of the research that enriched this book.

Andrew Dresser, for reading through a draft of the book and making valuable suggestions for revisions.

Kathryn Hasan, whose incalculable generosity provided bread and butter for my table — and more — while I wrote. Without her assistance this book would still be just a nice idea.

Patricia Heinicke Jr., of WordShine, who copyedited the manuscript. She ferreted out the weak spots of this book — point by point, sentence by sentence, word by word. Through her talent, this book was tightened in its very nooks and crannies, in all the places I hadn't dared to look alone.

Georgia Hughes, editorial director with New World Library, a.k.a. *editor extraordinaire*. She found the book, loved the book, and then judged it point-blank. I think that editing a book is something akin to judging a new mother's infant child: "Cute kid, but what's up with that *nose?*" Somehow Georgia handled the job gracefully.

New World Library and staff, for rolling the dice with me despite the long odds and, more generally, for maintaining a stage for healing and peace.

part 1

mapping
the road
ahead

introduction

wherein we meet
and fix our mark

When the mind is still... it returns to itself, and
by means of itself ascends to the thought of God.

— Saint Basil the Great[1]

the journey before you is an ancient exploration unlike any other. It is not a journey through books or across time, and it cannot be approached through ordinary learning methods. Meditation is a form of self-exploration in which the explorer shifts perspective, moving from a fixation on external affairs to a focus on internal seeking. The methods vary as much as do personal beliefs. Yet the experiences attained through consistent practice bridge the boundaries between religion, race, gender, and even time itself. The inner mind is the same today as it was when Buddha and Christ walked the Earth.

I have written this book in a style that will allow even the most ordinary person to experience the extraordinary benefits of meditation. You need not be a saint, prophet, or mystic; all you need is a determination to live a more fulfilling life, a small amount of time, and a spirit of exploration and discovery. From these simple commitments flow the experiences that serve as catalysts, carrying your learning to deeper levels of understanding. In the beginning nothing matters but your desire — the desire to expand your grasp of self-awareness and to face life with unflinching curiosity, to become innocent like a newly born child, touching and tasting the environment for the first time.

So before we go any further, let's pause and look at what meditation *appears to be,* just as an infant first examines the new world. From this viewpoint of exploration and fresh awareness, what does meditation look like?

Picture a man meditating cross-legged on a mat. His eyes are closed, his back is straight, and his shoulders, neck, and head are squarely in line with each other. His breathing is relaxed and regular, and his forehead and face are serene. Aside from his rising and falling chest, he is perfectly still, apparently deeply relaxed. He exudes a sense of focus, silence, and peace. He appears at peace with himself, at peace with all activity around him. He has entered a deep state of meditation and is experiencing a profound state of awareness.

Now add a new dimension to this picture: you and a

scientist are working in a lab, studying the effects of meditation on this man. For reference, you have a small arsenal of studies and books — some relating directly to meditation, others to general psychology, and still others to stress and sickness and the mounting evidence of the connection between mind and body. You also have the requisite tools for probing your subject's physiological responses — an electroencephalograph (EEG) to measure brainwaves, an electrocardiograph (EKG) to measure the heart's activity, and some test tubes and syringes to collect blood samples for analysis.

Perhaps your research would note some of the things scientists have already observed while studying meditation. During meditation there is a decrease in blood pressure, the heartbeat and respiration slow, and less oxygen is consumed while less carbon dioxide is produced. An EEG notes an increase in alpha wave activity in the brain (associated with serenity), and the levels of lactate in the blood plunge (high levels are associated with stress). Besides these immediate effects there are also long-term physiological changes.

For instance, a study in the medical journal *Psychosomatic Medicine* found that subjects in a meditation group had lower concentrations of lipid peroxides than did those in a control group of nonmeditators.[2] Some evidence suggests that the amount of these fatty substances directly correlates to biological age, and by extension to a rash of age-related diseases. Additionally, the authors cite other research that has shown that meditation decreases stress, which has been linked with diseases such as coronary heart disease, cancer, and rheumatoid arthritis.

In another study, Dr. Lawrence R. Murphy of the National Institute for Occupational Safety and Health reviewed literature on "worksite stress-management intervention." Murphy found that of all the stress management techniques studied, "Meditation produced the most consistent results."[3] This conclusion has significant implications, especially when coupled with a mounting body of related studies that suggest high levels of stress may play a key role in the development of certain diseases.

As more connections are made between meditation and health, a striking image is emerging. Either of itself, or in combination with corresponding changes in habit, diet, and general outlook on life, meditation is now being strongly associated with better physical and psychological health and longevity.

Researchers and physicians have proposed that meditation may help alleviate the symptoms of a staggering list of ailments: hypertension, chronic pain, motion sickness, addictions, PMS and menopause discomfort, diabetes, irritable bowel syndrome, dermatological conditions, impotence, arthritis, insomnia, breast and prostate cancers, panic attacks, depression, and heart disease, among others. The ramifications of all this are incalculable, at both the individual and societal level. One thing is becoming clearer — meditation and its associated lifestyles yield very real benefits for practitioners.

The power of bringing the mind to stillness seems to spread throughout practitioners' lives like a systemic, healing balm. Improvements in physical and psychological health are only a small part of a larger reparation. Those who meditate regularly also report increased levels of creativity, productivity, and ability to concentrate. Philosophical views change and, it follows, so do relationships and social skills. Self-esteem rises, as does the ability to empathize, while negative emotions such as anger become increasingly intolerable. Overall, individuals become more productive, caring people, more capable of rendering valuable services to their communities.

Now, back in your lab with your own research subject, you might wonder, objective considerations aside, what this individual is experiencing *subjectively.* If you thumbed through a general psychology book to the section addressing meditation, it would likely be defined as an "altered state of consciousness." Reports by subjects participating in experiments, combined with the observable alterations in brain activity, have led to this definition.

Fine. But what *is* an altered state of consciousness?

More importantly, what is the *particular* altered state experienced during meditation? Something is happening during meditation; this much is clear. But science stops short in its efforts at probing beyond the surface issues. By its own methods, science is securely fastened to measurable phenomena. In the case of meditation, all that we can witness and record are but *consequences* of the practice; they do not *define* it. In essence, they are side effects.

This holds true for the physical effects of meditation as well as the personality shifts experienced in meditative practice. All the things we can see and touch and measure are like ripples spreading out from a rock's splash in a calm pond. They move out from a central event, following the event but not causing it. Studying the effects of meditation leads to little understanding of what is going on under the surface. The best that such study can do is demonstrate that something must be producing the effects. If there are ripples on a once-smooth pond, something must have caused them.

Despite the limitations of a scientific scrutiny of meditation, scientific observation is now helping us understand this ancient practice. These days, spiritual teachers are regularly relating their own theories back to actual scientific research, rightly or wrongly, and researchers are becoming increasingly interested in probing the mystery of self-awareness. Modern science and medicine have

encouraged popular interest in meditation by document-
ing the observable phenomena associated with it, namely
the health benefits. They have also lent favorable models
for learning and evaluation, helping to counter some of
the negative stereotypes associated with the practice.
When we examine meditation fairly, we can see that it has
much to offer to a needy world, and that its pursuit does
not require us to sacrifice our fidelity to reason. This insight has been, in part, the gift of science to the meditative
community.

However significant the contribution of science,
though, there is a point beyond which spirituality and science cannot meaningfully connect. Meditation cannot be
learned through observation. It must be practiced to be understood. Hence the spirit of this book is one of active par-
ticipation, as opposed to pure intellectual study. To help
you participate, I have broken the text into thirty days of
practice. I encourage both beginners and those who already
meditate to commit to the full thirty days, regardless of
what happens, or doesn't happen, along the way.

Some people experience tremendous success very early
on, and for others it takes a while longer. Either way, you
will have to provide your own discipline, which can be
more difficult than simply following someone else's orders.
But discipline is crucial. It's pretty easy to slack off when
nobody's watching, which is the only possible way to go

astray when learning to meditate. If you commit your-self now to practicing regularly, every day, you'll be much more likely to tough it out, even if at first things seem difficult.

Back at the lab, still observing your test subject, you are now wondering what it is you cannot see; what is it the books don't answer and the tests don't reveal? Now, put the blood analysis and EEG reports aside, close your texts, and send the scientist home. This book is about direct experience. My goal is to take you from this external pic-ture of what meditation *looks* like to what it *feels* like; from the "poking and prodding," wondering and examining, straight into the meditative mind itself.

The experience is not as mysterious as at first it seems. Yet for all our efforts, it does stubbornly defy attempts to capture it within a test-tube. This is because it isn't an ex-ternal experience. We can examine our subject's test results and see his relaxed posture, poke him with needles, and analyze the level of lipid peroxides in his system. But what we can't see is that within his mind a most profound process is unfolding.

While our subject sits silently, apparently unmoved and experiencing nothing unusual, a powerful encounter is taking place within him. It is as if he has tapped some unseen force that runs like a river underneath the level of ordinary perception. He has a sense of connection to a larger body, and a view of life as an unbroken continuum, extending far beyond our own definitions of reality as a strictly physical phenomenon.

People have many different reasons for wanting to learn to meditate. Perhaps in the beginning they want only to have a little lipid peroxide reduction or enjoy the other health benefits to be wrought through meditation. Perhaps they desire the positive personality traits that meditation nurtures, traits that in turn can lead to stronger, more peaceful relationships, financial success, and so on. Others may find that through meditation their levels of creativity boom; people who never thought they could paint may find themselves painting, people who never thought they could write may find themselves writing, and people who have struggled for years to learn to play a musical instrument may suddenly open up to a flow everyone would recognize as inspired. Some even claim to have developed "psychic" abilities or other paranormal powers through meditation.

But beyond all of these diverse incentives lies a single motivation: a mystical awareness that can be touched through the practice of meditation. The feelings generated by the experiences one has during meditation tend to be of wholeness, peace, and well-being. A quietness creeps into the lives of those who actively pursue meditation, as well as a basic, primitive clarity. Sometimes, too, there are

11

feelings of outright joy or a sense that one is awakening to a larger Life.

However this "altered state" is interpreted or whatever its physical and psychological manifestations, this mystical awareness is the extraordinary feature that transports the practice beyond the field of normal human experience, into the realm of the mystics. It opens us up to an entirely new viewpoint of life, affording us a glimpse into the root of human existence. This is the real power of stillness. It is the stone that causes the ripples. Touching it requires one to pass beyond all the effects and search out the heart of the practice. This is a journey that takes us into the essence of our lives — into the deepest collective mind of humanity, which is also, I have come to believe, the very mind of God.

<u>nuts and bolts</u>

minding the
basics

The only thing you need to begin with —
and to go on with —
is commitment to regular practice.

— Doriel Hall[4]

for some the word *meditation* sparks images of bald Tibetan monks sitting atop Himalayan peaks, engaged in mysterious feats of mind over matter, perhaps levitating or saving laundry money by drying damp sheets with their own body heat. Others associate meditation with the 1960s — with protests, social change, and groups of friends exchanging abstract verse.

Besides these stereotypical images of meditation, add a fundamentalist or two to the mix, preaching that meditation is actually the "devil's work," practiced by heathens, unbelievers, or perhaps even demons. Many of these judgments and stereotypes come from people who have no experience whatsoever with meditative practice. In fact, every major religion has had prophets or teachers who practiced meditation as a part of their daily routine. Christianity, Islam, and Judaism all have rich mystical traditions, in large part generated from insights gathered through meditation or similar practices.

As I see it, a part of exploring meditation involves examining your beliefs and taking them to a higher level. No one need set aside religious faith to undertake meditation. You don't have to abandon your church and join your friendly neighborhood cult. You don't need to "drop out" to "tune in." Most religious traditions work well with the meditative lifestyle.

The way to begin is to be willing to challenge yourself and your mindset in order to evolve. In part this involves setting aside the stock definitions of meditation so that we can root out the reality of the practice. The first goal then is to attempt the impossible: to define the word *meditation*.

what is meditation?

Although no one who has taken meditation seriously could expect to answer this question fully, those who are learning still ask it. And the answers they get often leave them dissatisfied. Meditation is not easily defined because the experience one can attain through practicing it is beyond ordinary human awareness. In the beginning we have no reference point, nothing to which we can compare the experience. So defining meditation is a little like trying to explain the color blue to people who have never seen it. It would be much easier to simply point to the sky so that they could see for themselves. Without this immediate experience, definitions leave one little more than curious.

One simple definition of meditation is "the practice of stillness and silence." A person sets aside some private time, sits down, and attempts to remain perfectly still — both in body and in thought. In some types of meditation a person will choose a word, sentence, or image to focus on during meditation — a single "thought" to focus on as a replacement for all the other thoughts that normally fill human awareness. In other meditative practices, the emphasis is on letting *no* thoughts take root but instead letting thoughts drift in and out of awareness, like clouds crossing a blue sky. However, the uniting element underlying most forms of meditation is essentially identical: one's focus on the physical is gently de-emphasized and redirected toward the mental or metaphysical, the mind or spirit.

To better understand how this works, let's consider sensory deprivation tanks. A sensory deprivation tank is a chamber filled with saltwater. Inside the tank a person floats in the water, which has been warmed to about body temperature. The top is closed, sealing the person in darkness and quiet. The warm water deprives the body of tactile input (touch), the darkness suppresses sight, and the tank at least muffles exterior sounds. The result is an experience of the self as a "free awareness" or "pure consciousness," as it is often called, a mind aware of its existence independent of the physical world and body.

Meditation leads in the same direction. We find a relatively quiet place to sit still and close our eyes to the world for a while. The senses, with some major limitations, are curtailed from inputting data for the mind to consider. Our lack of physical movement reduces the sensation of tactile awareness; our closed eyes remove the physical from our sight; and a quiet corner becomes a haven from sounds likely to trigger inner dialogues to distract us. *Stillness and silence.*

Eventually, through the practice of keeping still, our thoughts quiet and we begin to realize that we are spiritual beings temporarily experiencing life as physical beings in a physical world. Meditation opens up the limited nature of our everyday thinking and our accustomed definitions of who and what we are, revealing an inner world, previously invisible. But this experience cannot truly be understood through definitions or descriptions; indeed, this experience is itself the best definition of meditation. Hence the problem: Meditation is an experience, so to understand it you will have to experience it for yourself.

theory

Aside from attempting to define medita
achieve better intellectual footing by examin
phy common to many forms of the practice ___gine, for
the sake of understanding, that you are actually two very
different individuals. One of these selves you know well. It
is the self you are familiar with, the self that wakes each
morning to go to school or work or play. You define this self
by a body and a name and a system of personal values,
desires, likes, and dislikes. In fact, for the bulk of your life
this is probably the only self you have been aware of. Some
people call this the "little self," the "I," or the "ego." It is
identity based on individual physical existence and a sense
of disconnection from spiritual awareness. From our normal
perspective, this ego-self seems to comprise all that we are.

But there is another Self within each of us, which goes
by many different names: Soul, Spirit, Love, Peace, Self,
Mind (in the abstract, or intangible, sense, as opposed to
the physical brain), and so on. What this Self is can't be
taught through words; it is only through experience that
its nature is understood. Perhaps you know your Self
through a sense of its weakness: perhaps you feel that
something is missing in your life — you feel a little empty
hole near your core. This feeling might be so obscure you
can't exactly say what the problem is, what's missing, or

why you somehow feel incomplete even when things are going well. There is an emptiness and a feeling that no matter what you do, life holds no complete satisfaction. Nothing you do quenches this weird, restless sense of deprivation.

Usually people aren't even aware of this feeling, but every now and then it threatens to surface and we struggle to suppress it because we have no real answer to the problem. Maybe the feeling comes in a "blue" day or, at the opposite end of the spectrum, in severe depression. Occasionally it can be glimpsed just beneath a sudden rash of exciting new goals enlisted to make life seem fresh again and to stifle this sense that our lives are somehow incomplete.

My own belief is that most of our dark emotions are actually the result of a deep denial of our spiritual Self in favor of the little self, the ego-self. By this view, the only ultimate answer to suffering is to become increasingly aware and accepting of our spiritual Self. Hence the value of meditation — a form of communion whereby we do just that. The spiritual Self is gradually acknowledged and accepted, and so the fulfillment each of us has sought is finally attained.

This description of human awareness goes beyond the simple definition of meditation as "the practice of stillness and silence," and it is the premise upon which the philosophical portions of this book are based. Sitting still is merely the form used to achieve it.

Beyond this philosophical view, the primary incentive for practicing meditation is really very simple — it allows us to stop, sit down, and finally discover and appreciate the beauty and joy of life beyond personal expectations and circumstances. This seems easy advice to give but difficult advice to follow, for it is part of human nature to always seek another set of circumstances in order to be happy. Look around and you might notice that many people are dissatisfied with their work and, judging by the divorce rate (about 50% according to the U.S. Census Bureau), even more so with their lovers. All too often our response to dissatisfaction is to pack up and move on. At every job I've ever held, one of the greatest problems the management faced was the constant coming and going of its employees. Everyone seems to think the grass will be greener over yonder. We think we would be happy if only we had more money, or if we were famous, or better looking. The fact remains, though, that upon winning the lottery, a sad poor person would be instantly transformed into nothing more than a sad rich person. So what's the use?

It takes some courage and honesty to finally come to grips with the fact that our sadness is actually self-generated. In meditation we aren't searching for yet another change of circumstance, with another phony promise of satisfaction. We aren't looking to move away to greener pastures but instead to nurture the lawn we already own, to make *it* greener. If your grass is brown now, moving to a new home with a fresh lawn wouldn't help much. Pretty soon your faulty gardening skills would catch up with it, and you would be stuck with the same problem from which you were hoping to escape. Through meditation we learn to stop seeking fulfillment outside of us, and seek instead the deeper fulfillment of communion with our Self.

learning to learn

In studying meditation we can deal only with the practice, understanding that the experience will never be accurately communicated, just as the concept of *blue* would be impossible to grasp apart from experience. In one sense, learning the particulars of meditative practice is very simple, a lot like any learning endeavor. Yet in another, less definable way, learning to meditate requires us to adopt a new set of rules for the learning process itself. We need a new model for learning because these lessons lead us along a path that runs in the opposite direction from what we have already learned.

My initial meditative practice involved a lot of guess-work. So will yours. In large part learning to meditate requires experimentation. As you practice, your experiences will lend you a clearer understanding of the learning process. Keep this in mind as you read this book and practice the meditations. Certain ideas may not be clear to you at first. However, by attempting to apply them you will acquire a firmer understanding of how they work.

At first you may have no idea what you are supposed to be looking for, what you are supposed to be experiencing. You may not even know how to begin. And so you may experience a sense of disorder or aimlessness. One of the most common thoughts that run through a person's mind the first time they try to meditate is, "Am I meditating yet?" It may seem that nothing is happening. On top of this, meditation teachers tend to communicate in abstract terms. So it's not surprising that frustration is a standard complaint of beginners. Don't be discouraged if at first nothing seems to happen. In all learning there is an initial period of *not understanding*.

In our society we are very accustomed to learning *facts*. Two plus two equals four — either you understand that or you don't. It's a fact that need be learned only once. And we're not alone in this type of thinking. For instance, the Eastern concept that there is a moment of perfect understanding, often referred to as "enlightenment," is a reflection of this same belief — that all learning entails the dry intake of information, or that facts are either understood ot. Meditation, however, is a learning process gradually. This is not to say that there is no mal moment of enlightenment," but for now it might be more helpful to think of meditation as you would exercise: the longer you do it, the stronger and more fit you get. You have to meditate regularly to achieve the benefits. If you exercise once a year it's not going to help you a whole lot. Meditate regularly for a year and the figure you see in the mirror will appear subtly different: clearer, more focused, at ease. Meditate regularly for five years and the transformation will likely be striking. And, remarkably, the change continues to accrue. Many people dismiss this in favor of the search for the perfect moment, yet it is one of the most beautiful aspects of a disciplined practice: there appears to be no end to the progress one can make. So don't be too quick to judge your progress. Let your commitment be to regular practice as opposed to any sort of defining moment.

Conversely, some people have powerful moments of mystical awareness right from the start. They are able to make an intuitive leap and open up to the meditative experience almost immediately. More often, people experience one of the shades of gray between total confusion and clear understanding. There are breakthroughs and frustrations, and either can come at any point during the process. Learning to cope with mood swings is the best ability a newcomer can develop. It is far more important than having what one feels is a strong start. Some people who have weak experiences in the beginning go on to become excellent students, well grounded and committed to the long haul. Their advancement unfolds neatly over a period of years, providing a cumulative base upon which steady growth can be nurtured. Those who have glorious beginnings may find it difficult to continue later when the "glitter" fades. The quality of your beginning experience, however, will not predict whether you will ultimately fail or succeed. The main point is that you cannot let *apparent* success or *apparent* failure dictate your practicing regimen.

There will be long periods along the way when things don't seem to be going well. These can be difficult to cope with. Along this path there will be experiences of great joy and others of great dread, and plenty of frustration in between. If you revel too greatly in the successes, the failures can become almost unbearable. There will be times when the very last thing in the world you want to do is sit down and meditate. At other times it will be your first priority. The advanced meditator learns that such experiences simply come and go. The only choice you have is in how you deal with them. Anyone who expects to make real progress needs to learn that fighting against such varying experiences only induces unnecessary struggle. Letting pain and failure go means letting success go as well. If you can focus on the meditation and not on the *quality* of the meditation, you will emerge stronger, more capable, and better balanced.

In meditation, striking a balance during all the ups and downs is what counts. This balance is the only true measure of success in meditation, and it serves as an excellent learning paradigm: regardless of how you feel, you sit down daily at your regular time, you experience whatever it is you happen to experience, and then you move on with your life until it is time to sit down again.

how to use this book

This is a book of ideas and practice. It is divided into thirty sections, one to be considered each day so that it will take you about a month to work through. Read only one section a day, and then try the meditation for that day. For best results, resist the temptation to jump ahead, skip over days, or read the whole text straight through without practicing. Some of the ideas presented in later portions will make better contextual sense with several weeks of practice behind you.

Each daily section is organized into two parts. The first part discusses topics related to meditation and spirituality, and the second, titled "Stop and Practice," explains the specific meditation practice to apply that day (with the exception of two "free days," which will allow you the opportunity to practice however you choose). Many of the exercise instructions are short and easy to remember, but if you have difficulty recalling them, you can have someone read them to you as you sit quietly. Or you might try recording the "Stop and Practice" sections as you read them aloud. Then you can play back the instructions while you practice.

As for the philosophical discussions, I recommend that you read through and consider these sections whether or not you agree with the particulars. Read them, consider them, use what is helpful to you, and file the rest away. My purpose isn't to replace your beliefs with mine but to help you to distinguish useful ideas — those that are conducive to happiness and learning — from ideas that limit your ability to transcend traditional human notions about God or Spirit. This can be very challenging because we can reason only from within the framework of our own personal beliefs. As a result, growth is often experienced as a threat.

Be willing to bear through such moments of challenge. Always be willing to question your own beliefs, keeping in mind that changing scenery marks progress along any road. As you travel you'll need to take an inventory of long-standing assumptions and evaluate your ideas, asking of each: "Is this dog dead, or is it just sleeping?" In other words, are my beliefs dead-ends, or can I use them as a springboard to real spiritual experience? We'll need to poke them with a stick to find out. This is not always so pleasant; some dogs bite.

Above all other considerations, please keep in mind that nothing in this book is gospel. I am sure plenty of dogmatism lurks among these pages, but if it is the fate of the dogmatic to blindly pursue their own folly, then I am, and intend to remain, happily bewitched. So never trust theology of any sort, including mine, as a be-all and end-all guide. Develop your own firsthand understanding through practice. Experience is the only way to establish real trust and gain real insights. In my view, blind faith should never substitute for experience except as a temporary measure. Practice and explore, practice and experience, and then practice, practice, practice some more.

posture and positions

How to sit during meditation has been emphasized again and again throughout the various meditative traditions, but I think it is a secondary matter. There aren't any magical positions, and in the beginning comfort is paramount. Many give up meditation after only a few sessions, complaining that their backs, ankles, or legs hurt. This is because they have been told that they must adopt positions that just don't work for them. This seems to me like putting the cart before the horse.

I encourage you to try any sitting position that you find comfortable, adjusting as you practice to suit your needs. Sit in a way that helps you to feel relaxed, keeping in mind the following points:

- Sit up when you meditate if at all possible. Reclined positions tend to induce withdrawal, whereas sitting up will help keep you alert. Despite appearances, meditation is not a passive, sleepy state. If you have a physical disability that prevents you from sitting erectly, simply do your best to adopt a position as close to the ideal as possible, or check with your physician for advice. As a last resort meditation can be performed in a partially or fully reclined position. Do what you need to do.

- Avoid the tendency to slouch. Keep your back as straight as is comfortable for you. Ideally, your spine, neck, and head should be in a vertical line, extending from your tailbone to the base of your skull. Theories differ as to why keeping your back straight is important, but one of the more obvious reasons is that good posture, like sitting up, helps to keep you alert, and in the long run it's certainly easier on the back.

• Place your hands however you feel most comfortable, either clasped together or held apart. Most people either rest them in their laps or somewhere along their thighs. The palms may be up or down. Remember, there is no magic meditative position.

Here are four popular positions you can experiment with:

the perfect position

A cross-legged position, the perfect position provides excellent stability without requiring the flexibility of the related lotus positions (see below). It may be performed on a blanket on the floor or on a bed.

1. Sit on a pillow or two so that when you cross your legs at least one of your knees is resting on the floor or at least is very close to it. I usually use two standard bed pillows.

2. Pull one foot in as close as possi
   posite thigh.
3. Lift the other foot and place it o
   opposing calf.
4. Check your posture to ensure you
   straight, as recommended above.
5. During long meditations switch leg positions
   occasionally.

the lotus position

Simultaneously the most stable and the most difficult position, the lotus takes the perfect position one step further. In the half lotus, instead of resting one foot on the opposite *calf,* you rest one foot on the opposite *thigh.* In the full lotus, you rest *both* feet on their opposite thigh. This is tough for all but the most flexible people. I recommend you try the perfect position before you try this one.

the seated (or egyptian) position

This position is probably the most comfortable one for beginners. You will need a straight-backed, armless chair or low stool and a pillow, if you like, for lower back support (or for additional padding to sit on).

1. Sit in the chair with your feet flat on the floor. If you like, use a pillow wherever it helps you

feel more comfortable, either behind your back or underneath your buttocks.

2. Check your posture to ensure your back is straight.

the buddhist position

This is another easy position for beginners. The most common complaints about it are pain in the shins, ankles, and thighs, and the fact that unless you get the position just right, the legs tend to go numb quickly. This should not be a problem in the beginning, however, as our meditations will be short.

The Buddhist position is performed on a flat surface such as a padded yoga mat on the floor. Besides a floor mat or some other type of padded surface, you will also need a pillow; if you find you enjoy this position, you can purchase a round, firm meditation pillow especially designed for this position. Such pillows can be found easily enough by searching for "meditation pillows" on the Internet, inquiring through your local Buddhist church, or checking with a bookstore that specializes in spirituality.

1. Kneel with your shins and the tops of your feet flat on the floor and your legs separated enough to allow a pillow to fit between them. Unless you are violating the laws of anatomy,

the soles of your feet should be facing up with
your toes pointing straight back.

2.   Slide a firm pillow or two between your legs
     and sit down

3.   Check your posture to ensure that your back
     is straight.

time and place matters

Beyond posture and positions, it's also important to consider how long, when, and where you should meditate. Ultimately these are personal decisions you will need to make
for yourself. However, for now the following guidelines
will help you get started.

As you read this book you will be practicing once or
twice a day, as indicated in each section. I recommend you
establish a regular time each day for your meditations,
preferably in the morning and/or evening. Your morning
practice should be undertaken as soon as possible after you
wake up. Be sure to allow ample time to get comfortable
and enjoy a leisurely pace. It may be difficult for you to
relax into your meditation if you are concerned about getting to work on time.

Your evening meditation, in contrast, should be undertaken as close to your bedtime as is feasible, keeping in

mind that you should avoid meditating when you are overly tired. There aren't any hard-and-fast rules, so you can do your evening meditation earlier if you prefer. The important thing is to divide your practice into morning and evening sessions. Pick a time that works for you, and then try to meditate at about the same time each day. It should be a time when you can briefly slip away from whatever responsibilities fill your days.

The amount of time you spend in meditation will vary according to your own needs and desires. In the "Stop and Practice" portions of this book I suggest how long to spend meditating each day, but these suggestions are merely guidelines. If you have had some experience with meditation, by all means extend the amount of time to meet your needs. For those just getting started, I recommend that you follow the suggestions until you feel entirely comfortable with longer meditations.

The exercises in this book begin with short meditations and then gradually work up to longer sessions. The reason for this is that you will meditate only if you enjoy doing so. It's a simple fact. Although meditation is a pleasurable experience, at first there can be strong resistance. This is particularly true if the beginner attempts steps before being prepared. "Slow but steady" is wise advice that holds true during all stages of spiritual advancement. Attempting long meditations before you are ready can actually *increase* your resistance.

Another reason for shorter initial meditations is that if you sit for longer periods at the beginning, you will likely find yourself caught up in mundane thought processes, which is not meditating at all. Quality, not quantity, is most desirable, and it is best not to get into the lax habit of considering your meditation periods as times you set aside to "think about things." Instead, give your all to the short periods recommended. If you sit around thinking for hours, you may as well be watching television. Let your practice periods be devoted to the recommended meditation. You can think about things all you like for the rest of the day.

Besides a designated time, you will also need a relatively quiet place where you can be alone. This is particularly important in the beginning, when distractions of all sorts will plague you. Sometimes when you are trying to meditate the world doesn't seem to care — the kids are running through the house, the spouse is wailing, sirens are screaming, the whole of hell has broken loose, and it sounds as if they're having a reunion in your living room! Try not to get frustrated. There really isn't any way around such distractions. Still, it's important to pick the best time and the quietest place for you and to let those around you know you are going to be meditating. This should help to alleviate at least some of the exterior noise.

With these "nuts and bolts" of meditation in mind, remember that meditation is not about hiding out, sitting in some fancy position with perfect posture, defining the word or the practice, or any of the correlated basics. It is about finding a quiet place that already exists within you, like a sculptor seeking an invisible shape that already exists within a plain block of wood. The idea is to carve away the extras to uncover the art within. Thus meditation is not an *adding to,* but a *taking away.* In meditation one seeks to experience the basic mind apart from self-concepts. All the rules and guidelines set down as a part of learning to meditate become added images that, in the end, will themselves be shed. This process at first seems contradictory: we need to add on so we can take away. We need a repertoire of tools and skills designed to dismantle what has already been established; and then we dismantle the tools and skills. We use words and ideas in our practicing only to lead us beyond them.

When you are ready, find your quiet nook and read through the next section, "Day 1." Be sure to try the corresponding exercise outlined near the end, a simple introduction to meditative practice. It is my hope that through your own practice, you will be able to find and cultivate a place of peace within yourself. As with so many who have discovered the peace of meditation, my profoundest desire is to share this experience with others. So sit back and relax; the journey before you is a quiet one, and it begins the moment you are ready. So turn the page, and let's get started!

part 2

the journey

begins

a thirty-day

workbook

day 1

thought webs
the importance of focus

You can't stop the birds from flying back and forth over your head, but you can stop them from nesting in your hair.

— Saint Francis[1]

during the early stages of my own practice I coined a phrase summing up both my difficulties and successes practicing meditation: "catching the thread." Our minds are busy places that don't appear to contain anything but our own thoughts — words and images but nothing more interesting. However, there is a spark in the mind, even amidst the ordinary busyness, that leads us further. I likened this tiny spark to the end of a thread blowing unnoticed in the wind of my thoughts. Spotting and seizing this thread is difficult at first, but when you first succeed you will recognize it, and each time you succeed thereafter it will become easier for you to find. Furthermore, this thread acts as a sort of guide rope, enabling you to follow its length to deeper meditative experiences.

When addressing meditation we are talking about *mind,* and so we must deal with our thoughts. Consider your mind's content for a moment. The human thought process is not graceful. From morning till night our thoughts clatter through our minds like elephants dancing the two-step tango in a glassware shop. Even trained minds cannot maintain a single, simple thought for long. If you were able to record all of your thoughts — both the spoken and the silent ones — for a day, or even an hour, you may very well be horrified at what you would hear during playback. Your thoughts would probably sound like the ramblings of a madman, shifting from one topic to the next with no concern whatsoever for reason or elegance — zipping along at an astounding rate, jumbled and disorganized, and in the end comprising not much more than idle chitchat.

Anyone who has tried to focus on a single thought understands this well. In writing this book, for instance, I have found that I have to constantly stop and read over what I just wrote only moments before because I have already forgotten what I wanted to say. In fact, a big part of any writer's life is simply learning to focus.

Similarly, most people who meditate begin to realize that their minds are totally disorganized and undisciplined.

Our thoughts run on and on, seemingly of their own vo-
lition, one thought inspiring the next, and we may sift
through hundreds each hour. So our minds, if viewed objectively, appear about as cohesive as warm Jello splattered
across hot cement. This endless inner chatter makes up
what we think of as our entire inner world. What we don't
realize, though, is that this is only surface stuff, like little
ripples on a vast ocean of water.

As you begin to meditate you will very likely begin to
gain a sense of the disarray of your thinking process. This
can be uncomfortable. Your mind and thoughts may even
appear to speed up while you are trying to meditate, never
allowing you a moment's peace. What you need to remember is that the meditative experience has nothing to
do with what you identify as your thoughts. As long as you
are responding to your thoughts, the experience you are
seeking will remain obscure.

The thread you are attempting to catch exists beyond
ordinary thoughts, and you will most likely first glimpse it
during the brief moments of quiet *between* the chatter of
your thoughts. What you are trying to do in meditation is
to loosen your identification with your thoughts so that
you can sink beneath them into a quiet sphere, like diving
beneath the surface of a pool.

One way to do this is to focus exclusively on one
thought or one word during meditation, which helps to

loosen your identification with the rest of the chatter. "Focus sentences" (or "focus words") are similar to mantras (see Days 6 and 7), except that they need not be repeated continuously, as mantras generally are, and are rarely spoken aloud. You use a focus sentence as a casual reference during meditation, repeating it as often as you like, but never in a rushed or strained manner. If it helps, think of the focus sentence as the center of a daisy, while the petals of the flower are all your other thoughts. Sometimes your mind will get lost staring at all the pretty petals, but your practice is to consistently return your attention to the center of the flower: your focus sentence. In this way the intense hold of your thoughts is gently loosened, and your focus naturally turns inward.

stop and practice

Today you are going to try one of the simplest forms of meditation there is. In the meditation you won't be attempting to go beyond your thoughts, fight against them, or experience anything in particular, but instead you will simply try to get a feel for letting them come and go without attachment. We are not our thoughts. Our thoughts are only products of our mind. They pull at us and enchant us incessantly, trapping us in a mental word web. We feel as if we are one with them, as if we are *our* thoughts. Today, quite simply, you are going to question this belief.

Beyond all our thoughts but still within our minds, there is a quiet place, much as a busy city might have a tranquil park within its boundaries. To those living in the rush of city life, such a park may go unnoticed as they speed right past it without so much as a sideward glance. The busy inhabitants have no time to stop and explore. But for those who do, great rewards await.

Once today set aside about five minutes of your time to rest your body and mind. Don't expect too much. Don't even try to understand the purpose behind the exercise. You need not feel stress over anything in this practice. Don't worry about whether or not you are doing the exercise correctly. Just relax and do your best to apply the following:

1. Sit down, make yourself comfortable, and close your eyes.
2. Take several deep, relaxing breaths. Feel the air fill your lungs from the bottom up, holding it

for a few seconds before you exhale in one long, extended stream.

3. Relax your body. Take a few moments to get a sense of relaxation in your muscles, letting all the tension drop away as if it were flooding out of you and into the air. Relax your neck and shoulders, your arms and hands, your chest, stomach, and back, and finally your thighs, calves, and feet.

4. Now think to yourself, "I think, but I am not my thoughts." This is your focus sentence. Use it as a focus for your meditation, repeating as often as needed to keep your mind focused on these words instead of the chatter.

5. Between repetitions of the focus sentence, try, as best you can, to observe your thoughts without interacting with them. For instance, if a thought about work occurs to you, you might be tempted to dwell on it or to follow its course to another related thought such as plans for the weekend, when you don't have to work. Instead, when you notice that you are engaging with a thought, stop, note the thought, and then return your attention to

the focus sentence. Sometimes you will be successful and sometimes not; in either case another thought will follow. Just continue the process with each new thought.

6. Whenever you realize that you've forgotten about your meditation and have let your mind engage with a thought — which is likely to be much more often than not — interrupt your train of thought by repeating your focus sentence, more than once if need be. Think it clearly in your mind, focus on it, and then return to the attempt to let your thoughts drift by passively. Be calm and gentle but also very firm with yourself on this point. Continually redirecting your focus to the meditation — letting thoughts rise and disappear — is the whole point of today's exercise. The function of the focus sentence is just to remind you of your meditation.

day 2

visualization
the mind's eye

*The mind is like a crazy monkey jumping
from one thing to another.*

— Patricia Monaghan and Eleanor G. Viereck[2]

Visualization is one of the most popular and practical meditation techniques a beginner can practice, and it makes for a great introduction to meditation. It is one of meditation's "thought tools," the specific practices, words, or images used to focus one's attention during meditation. And although some teachers argue that such practices are only added "stuff" and can detract from the true experience of meditation, as we begin we are so focused on the concrete particulars of daily life that we can hardly rise beyond them to any transcendent experience. Our thoughts, then, appear as an obstacle to the deeper experiences meditation aims to evoke. Because of this, an initial focus can help shape our ordinary thoughts into reflections of the deeper experience of the spiritual realm. Thus our thoughts, once seen as insurmountable barriers between Spirit and our awareness, actually open the door to this experience by presenting no opposition to it.

Most visualization practices involve simple images, or mind pictures, that provide the center of focus during meditation. For instance, during your meditation you could picture in your mind's eye Buddha, Christ, or some other teacher sitting beneath a tree while absorbed in perfect stillness and peace. Or you might prefer to picture yourself rapt in a similar state — or you could imagine a subtle light emanating from your chest and growing to encompass your whole body and mind.

Many such images are used in the various meditative traditions, and you can try a great number of them until you find one that suits you. Keep in mind that the particulars of the fantasy are not as important as their effects. Visualization is a sort of fiction meant to inspire real healing — and it succeeds when its full capacity is exercised. Choose an image that arouses a sense of peace, comfort, and holiness and play off it as much as you like, letting your entire mind engage with it until it becomes your solitary focus. Whatever the image, while you practice with it attempt to actually see it within your mind as clearly as possible, focusing on it while excluding extraneous thoughts. This is very definitely easier said than done, but, as with all the techniques we will try during the course of this book, persistent attempts will eventually yield success. For now, don't judge; just practice.

A secondary consideration is how long you should rely on visualization and similar aids to lead your meditations. I suggest you keep in mind that their usefulness is more a matter of *need* than of *time.* As long as a practice is useful in facilitating the experience you are seeking, it has a place.

Yet, as mentioned above, some maintain that the deepest meditation does not involve words or images but another experience, transcending human symbols altogether. I think that this is true, but as long as you find it difficult to achieve this higher state, your mind will remain prone to wandering. When brought in line with your purpose, an overactive imagination can act as a springboard instead of a hindrance to meditation. As deeper states are achieved, the thought tools become unnecessary and are easily discarded. Hence, the risk of attachment to such practices is minimal, and it is certainly outweighed by the potential benefit.

If you are serious about meditation, you should get used to using every bit of help available. If you are Christian, for instance, you should study Buddha's lessons on meditation, and if you are Buddhist, you would be wise to adopt Christ's teachings on forgiveness (the role of forgiveness in meditation will be addressed in Day 3).

Likewise, trying a variety of meditative techniques will broaden your understanding of the practice as a whole. Practicing visualization is not the best form of meditation for everyone, but everyone should at least try it. For those who find it effective, it can open up powerful feelings of devotion and peace.

stop and practice

Today we will try a very simple form of visualization. As you did yesterday, practice once today for five minutes. Even though it is only a very short meditation, consider this time an initial but vital investment toward what will eventually be an exponential increase in spiritual awareness.

1. As you did yesterday, sit down, close your eyes, take a few deep breaths, and relax your body. Allow your mind to quiet down a little. Many people who meditate have some beginning routine or ritual they go through prior to meditating; some people like to stretch, practice yoga, or work through a series of breathing exercises first. For now, at least practice

steps 1 through 3 from yesterday's instructions whenever you begin. (They won't be repeated.)

2. Now imagine a perfect, deep blue sky filling the whole landscape of your mind's eye, stretching upward and downward and extending out forever, with a golden, shining sun near the top. Try to picture this scene as clearly as you can.

3. Next, consider that the sky represents your mind — beautiful and broad and clear — and imagine that the sun is a source of great healing and nourishment. Keep your mind focused on this image for the remainder of your meditation, allowing your mind to bask in the healing rays of the sun.

4. Whenever your thoughts stray, gently recall the image. This will be difficult, but don't give in to frustration. In the beginning most people are able to concentrate only for a matter of seconds. Consider every effort to return your mind to your meditation a success.

day 3

forgiveness

a dynamic shortcut

Only my condemnation injures me.
Only my own forgiveness sets me free.

— A Course in Miracles[3]

m editation and forgiveness go hand in hand. Where you harbor anger, your meditations will be blocked. Where you forgive, you open up to the deeper experience this book describes. Learning forgiveness is a pivotal part of learning to meditate, and the practice of forgiveness will remain an important part of your spiritual experience in the long term.

Some people have spent years in meditative practice, searching for something they can never seem to touch. They might spend countless hours in the "practice of stillness and silence" without ever doing any of the real work of meditation — in part, learning forgiveness. Committing to regular meditation is vital, but it is only one step, and meditation is only one part of much larger spiritual practice. Remember, real results require real work. Forgiveness is the key to success that so many overlook. No mantra, no mind picture, no exercise will take you where a peaceful heart will. Learn forgiveness and your meditations will naturally deepen.

It is tempting to think that forgiveness comes when circumstances change: when the person you want to forgive makes amends or when you move on to other concerns or the score is evened in some way. But forgiveness is really self-work, or working to understand oneself and grow in spirit. It requires a commitment to questioning your own thinking process, as opposed to someone else's. If you hope to find peace, you must begin to realize that forgiveness involves a change in mindset, not in circumstance, and you alone are responsible for making that change. Forgiveness has to come from you; you can't hope for peace if you are relegating your responsibility to other people.

Adopting forgiveness is like changing the lens through which you view the world; it colors everything. You see nothing apart from your own mind — no injustice, no hatred, and no pain, but also no peace or joy or quiet. If you are looking through red-tinted glasses, everything will be colored red. Similarly, if your mind is clouded with anger and condemnation, this is what you will perceive. But this lesson goes even further. The key is to realize that you have the power to change this lens.

This recognition can finally open your life to powerful options previously unnoticed. It is a way of taking stock of your world and then acting to change the things that need changing. You take active charge of your mind and refuse to allow others to dictate what you should feel or how you should think. To me this is the only real power any of us can possess.

We can see how forgiveness operates by considering Isaac Newton's famous third law of motion, which states that "for every action there is an equal and opposite reaction." We all recognize this in physical terms: if you throw a ball against a wall it will bounce back to you. I believe this simple principle can be applied to a far broader range of experience, beyond ordinary physics; indeed, it seems that many physical laws are reflections of a greater orderliness underlying life in general. Applied to our thoughts, Newton's principle would suggest that if you hate, you will experience hatred. Anger projected out into the world will be returned in kind, just like a ball returning to its point of origin. This is expressed by the saying "What goes around comes around."

Yet a peaceful world, too, is a projection. It's not up to others to choose or decline your own peace of mind. Offer kindness to the world and you will find the justifications for it. Compassion, gentleness, and a quiet life are gardens that need to be planted before they can grow. Plant corn in a garden and corn will grow. Plant onions if you want onions to grow. If you don't like onions, then don't plant them. If you don't like animosity, then don't plant it. Doesn't this make sense, put into these simple terms? Then why be surprised by or upset with nature's simple laws?

If a person throws a ball against a wall and it bounces back and strikes that person in the eye, is it the ball's fault? Or should that person simply be a little more careful? The fact is, being angry with the ball won't help; *you* control the ball. Similarly, *you* choose how you view your circumstances and relationships.

Knowing this, each one of us needs to learn to become very selective about how we want our lives to look and feel. Plant the crops you would like to grow in your life, and don't plant those you'd rather not harvest. If you are an angry person, or an unhappy person, or an out-of-control person, you can change your experiences by changing the way you think of other people and the world in general. You don't *have* to hate, and you *can* learn to see people — even in their most insane moments — in a way that wishes them well, that hopes for healing, and that commands peace.

The practice of forgiveness makes clear the contrast between our old feelings of animosity and resentment and a new feeling of peace, and this contrast becomes a great teacher of forgiveness. When you see two distinct paths to travel on, learning becomes a simple matter of deciding which way you prefer. There is no other way to learn what forgiveness is, to understand what it means, and to experience the relief it offers as a replacement for all the turmoil we previously felt. Forgiveness is an experience, a lot like meditation; it is an opening of the heart so deep that the release it brings seems to go on forever. It is a gift you offer to others, but as you proceed and go deeper into its methodology, you finally begin to realize that forgiveness is also a gift you receive, something for yourself.

stop and practice

Today we are going to practice with a visualization technique geared toward forgiveness that has been borrowed from the spiritual teaching *A Course in Miracles*.[4] In it you will be practicing a version of Newton's theory that all actions produce reactions. Consequently, the more "heart" you are able to put into the exercise, the greater the results you will experience during your meditation.

Note, however, that there is a tendency to feel that

beginning meditative practices on forgiveness are deceitful. You may feel, for instance, that you are not really being honest by attempting to view in a positive light someone you sincerely dislike. But even if you feel this way, practice with the idea anyway. Be assured that this feeling is very common. Through it, try to gain a sense — even if it is only faint — of the possible relief true forgiveness could bring. This should be enough for now to motivate you to continue.

Begin the exercises with the relaxation you have been practicing in Days 1 and 2. After you are relaxed, try this meditation for about five minutes.

[Think] of someone you do not like, who seems to irritate you, or to cause regret in you if you should meet him; one you actively despise, or merely try to overlook. It does not matter what the form your anger takes. You probably have chosen him already. He will do.

Now close your eyes and see him in your mind, and look at him a while. Try to perceive some light in him somewhere; a little gleam which you had never noticed. Try to find some little spark of brightness shining through the ugly picture that you hold of him. Look at this picture till you see a light somewhere within it, and then try to let this light extend until it covers him, and makes the picture beautiful and good.

Look at this changed perception for a while, and turn your mind to one you call a friend. Try to transfer the light you learned to see around your former "enemy" to him. Perceive him now as more than friend to you, for in that light his holiness shows you your savior, saved and saving, healed and whole.

Then let him offer you the light you see in him, and let your "enemy" and friend unite in blessing you with what you gave. Now are you one with them, and they with you. Now have you been forgiven by yourself.

day 4

resistance
pulling up short

[Your ego is] like a familiar room built of thoughts...
You are secure in it, but to the extent that you are
afraid to venture outside, it has become a prison.

— Ram Dass[5]

Picture yourself mounted on horseback before a thick, wooded forest rising toward the foot of a mountain. The animal beneath you is powerful, built for long journeys such as the one before you. It has everything you need to successfully negotiate the woods and summit the peak above. Its enormous lung capacity ensures that it will go the distance; its loyalty makes it an ideal companion; its speed suggests that it will not waste time; and its height provides you with vantages that would be unavailable on foot.

It is very easy to imagine leaping onto such a horse, securing the reins, and charging off on your way. You can imagine the animal submitting and dutifully doing as it is instructed. You tell it to turn left, pull the reins, and the horse goes left. You nudge it with your heels, and the animal moves forward. You pull back, and it stops. Nor is it difficult to imagine yourself as an extension of the horse so that while you are riding, your will is joined with its will, and rider and animal operating as a single, mobile entity. If you try you can picture perfect harmony between horse and rider and an easy journey to your goal. We've all seen the movies.

Yet in the way of meditation this animal is no stallion, and such Hollywood images are rarely realistic. On this journey of meditation, the horse you ride is your own mind, and the peak is perfect peace.

So in order to achieve this objective you will have to learn to work in harmony with your mind and thoughts. At first your mind will not always do what you tell it to. Tell it to slow down, and it speeds up. Say "left," and it goes to the right. Knock it with your heels, and it stops cold and plants its feet like a stubborn mule waiting for dinner. At first the mind is just like this stubborn mule whose bray sounds remarkably like condescending laughter. And in turn, you might wonder, Is this the graceful machine intended to carry me home? For when we at first turn inward to face our inner Self, things can get a touch uncomfortable. Our path is not as neat or orderly as we would like, and we are heavily tempted to turn away from our journey, to throw up our hands and quit.

On the path of meditation you will have to surmount many obstacles. Their forms are many, but they are all really the same. They make the way seem difficult, sometimes even painful, and they cause delay. Some of them appear immediately upon embarking on the journey, while others will wait until you've gotten comfortable. You may have already encountered some of them. If not, prepare yourself to muscle through them. Just as a horse and rider might have to cross a river to get to where they want to be, so too will you have to overcome what lies between you and your goal. Here are a few of the more common hurdles you will have to navigate:

- *Physical discomfort.* When you sit down to meditate, at first you may find it physically painful. It doesn't seem that sitting quietly should cause any particular physical discomfort, and yet it does. If you are experiencing pain or tension while meditating, try a different sitting position or check your posture (see the "Posture and Positions" section in Part 1). Severe pain, of course, may be an indication of physical injury, in which case you should stop until you can consult a physician.

However, most aches, cramps, and other pains associated with meditation will subside as your body adjusts to sitting still.

- *The Poison-Ivy Syndrome.* Pain is not the only physical sensation that may be experienced during meditation. One of the most common feelings is the need to scratch, which, predictably, grows increasingly persistent the more you scratch. Virtually everyone experiences this to some degree. Go ahead and scratch when you must, but also make an effort to let these sensations disappear on their own. If you respond to every little itch, you won't be getting much from your meditations and you will end up feeling like a victim of poison ivy. This distraction will pass naturally as long as you don't make a big issue of it one way or another.

- *Drowsiness.* The only previous experience most of us have of sitting with closed eyes for an extended period is that of falling asleep. Because of this, the tendency to become drowsy during meditation is one of the most common, indeed insidious, obstacles along the path. So if the pillow you sit on is beckoning your head like a siren's song, be wary. It's better to entertain random thoughts than to drift into a passive, sleepy state. Once you allow drowsiness to become a regular part of your practice, you set up a pattern that can persist for months.

- *Breathlessness.* Some people feel they become short of breath when they meditate. But the fact is your body actually requires *less* oxygen during meditation. The sensation of breathlessness is a simple mind trick, much like an optical illusion. During meditation, breathe normally and don't worry about whether or not you are getting enough oxygen; *you are* (unless you are suffering from some illness that affects your respiratory process, in which case you would also be experiencing breathlessness when you aren't meditating). So if you are experiencing breathlessness only during meditation, recognize that it is just one more distraction you need to let go of. Without your interference, your body will take in all the air it needs.

- *Numbness.* Feelings of numbness during meditation are often first experienced in the extremities or, for some, the teeth. In fact you may feel as if you have physically "disappeared." This phenomenon causes some disorientation at first, and it can be frightening.

However, what you are experiencing when you feel this lack of sensation isn't actually numbness but a change in focus away from the body. Don't confuse it with the real numbness that occurs when circulation has been cut off from the legs and feet, which can occur when you are sitting cross-legged. A withdrawal from bodily awareness is different, and in fact it is a sign of progress.

- *Other physical sensations.* Reports of hot or cold flashes, tingling, and "energy surges," which may be experienced anywhere in the body but are most commonly reported as traveling along the spine, are all common enough. Some people experience them and some don't, but none of these feelings are anything to be concerned about. Don't let them dissuade you from continuing your meditative practice.

- *Visions.* Both auditory and visual hallucinations may occur during meditation, although these experiences are less common than the others. Some people hear bells, music, or other sounds; some people see visual images during meditation. These images are not the same as those used during visualization; they are more vivid, like dreams, and are sometimes signs of regression into hypnagogic, or pre-sleep, states. In most cases, such "visions" are nothing more than distractions, and they are certainly nothing to get excited about, one way or another.

Many other physical experiences are possible during meditation; those described above are only the most common. The most important thing is to recognize, now and fully, that our resistance to turning inward is enormous. It exists at a very primitive psychological level, just beneath our conscious minds. Be determined not to get sidetracked by the many little and large distractions you will inevitably encounter, whether or not they appear to be within your power to command. The best advice for overcoming any obstacle to meditation is to let all such experiences come and go without letting them dictate your practice, recognizing that they are not unattached, functionless symptoms but actually serve the purpose of distraction for its own sake, and are therefore best ignored.

stop and practice

For today's practice try the following exercise once for about five minutes:

1. Pick a visual image that represents for you peace and holiness, such as a teacher, a light, a feather, or some such.

2. Picture this image resting in your chest, approximately where your heart is. If you have chosen a teacher, imagine this teacher meditating in the same posture you are using. In your mind, draw as clear a picture as possible.

3. Now imagine that with each inhalation, or in-breath, the image grows slightly brighter, and with each exhalation, or out-breath, the image grows slightly larger. Do this until the image has grown to encompass your whole body.

4. Meditate on the feeling of unity with this image for the remainder of the practice. Feel as if it is imparting something very holy to you through your joining together.

day 5

resistance
mind traps

Man is two men; one is awake in darkness,
the other is asleep in light.

— Kahlil Gibran[6]

now that you have a little experience with meditation, it is important for you to be aware of some of the negative psychological states and traps that can be aroused. In addition to the physical distractions experienced during meditation, various emotions will be felt and new patterns of thought will form, both of which are inevitable considering that meditation is a mental experience. Emotions play a key role in most people's lives, and one of the main purposes of meditation is to break down stagnant thought patterns and form fresh ones, so it is not surprising that meditation can involve strong emotional experiences. Yet sometimes the emotions are painful, and sometimes the new thought patterns are just as hampering as the old ones. You will have to learn to recognize these states as mere distractions, just like the more concrete physical forms of resistance discussed yesterday. Here are four of the most common mind traps faced during meditation:

- *Anxiety.* Everyone deals with anxiety at some point. Later in this book the issue of fear, anxiety's big brother, will be addressed more thoroughly (see Day 23). For now I'll just reassure you — if you experience anxiety of any sort during meditation, first attempt to work through it however you can. This may involve reminding yourself that you are perfectly safe, or that your anxiety is irrational. Ask yourself to identify, in the clearest terms you can think of, what it is you are afraid of. Anxiety during meditation is usually associated with feelings of unworthiness (which is a lack of self-forgiveness), an inability to forgive others, or just a general discomfort with looking into your own mind. Some people think that there is something within them that is tainted, or even dangerous. These things are not true. All of the dark stuff is on the surface, and what you are seeking is far beyond it. Still, if you find you are unable to let go of anxiety, simply open your eyes until the feeling passes, and then return to your mediation. If anxiety becomes a major hindrance to your meditations, stop and seek the advice of a teacher.

- *Doubt.* For a while, doubt will be a companion: you may experience doubt about the efficacy of meditation, about whether or not it's right for you, about your own ability to learn the practice, and so on. There is a loud voice in each of us that objects to meditation and will do so again and again in many, many forms so long as we meditate, or until we advance to a point where this voice is silenced, or at least ignored. Everyone experiences this resistance to stillness and meditation to some degree. So be prepared to cope with it. And by all means, don't give up on meditation just because some form of doubt is urging you to quit. If you give your practice some time, you will learn that doubts, whatever their form, are really nothing more than a passing form of resistance. Eventually the powerful experiences of deep meditation will emerge, and all doubts will be quieted.

- *Depression.* Sometimes deep meditations are followed by feelings of depression. If you have a strong experience in meditation, the sadness that follows can be equally deep, and quite painful. For this reason, it is important to stabilize both your emotions and your progress so that extreme experiences at either end of the spectrum are more the exception than the rule. Learning to view periods of depression from a detached perspective is key to coping with all negative emotions.

In most cases, feelings of depression are mild. However, if you experience strong emotional reactions, it might be better for you to temporarily stop meditating and seek help from a qualified mental health care professional.

• *Power.* Meditation can produce both power, such as the ability to influence others through words, and the illusion of power, which is imagined power that exists only in one's mind. In either case, some people become enchanted by this sense of strength and attempt to use it to manipulate others, or else they become distracted with it and lose sight of their priorities. If you develop a sense of power, I recommend you use it only peacefully, to further the cause for peace. Don't use it to try and control other people, or to milk the world of all the worldly things you think you want. These manipulations will only cause you further pain, and if pursued strenuously, they can eventually lead to complete confusion and hopelessness.

This list may make it seem that meditation can cause some negative psychological states. The truth, however, is that meditation doesn't *cause* these states, it only arouses things that were already buried in the mind to begin with. To find psychological peace, you need to work out whatever meditation "digs up."

In life, circumstances and emotions constantly shift, but meditation can serve as a stable place that you will learn to rely on more and more as a comfort. You can expedite this learning by meditating consistently despite any obstacles you encounter along the way. Meditate when you are sick and also when you are well; meditate when you are tired, even if you have to prop yourself up against a wall. Meditate when you are happy, when you are sad, and even when your thoughts just won't stop, causing you to feel totally frustrated. Let doubts come and go, and meditate through it all. All of these experiences will pass: each shiver or itch or twist of fear, along with every busy thought that nags at you until you begin to believe you are only fooling yourself. Don't let these obstacles convince you that this is true. Move along, move along; whatever comes your way, just keep moving along.

stop and practice

Practice once today for five minutes with the following:

1. Become aware of a connection to the Earth beneath you. First, sense the place or places where your body meets with whatever you are sitting on, and then sense that place begin to dissolve. Imagine that you are an extension of your mat or chair and that it is an extension of the Earth. Try to feel the real, physical force of the Earth's gravity, to feel the physical connection between yourself and the Earth.

2. After you have sensed, however vaguely, some type of connection with the Earth, note that all people are similarly connected to it. Sense, then, your connection to all life through the Earth.

3. Finally, consider that it isn't the Earth that connects you to others, but another Force less definable. Try to sense this other Force within you, and meditate on it for the remainder of the five minutes.

day 6

the mantra

---

a word on words

For words, like Nature, half reveal
And half conceal the Soul within.

— Alfred, Lord Tennyson[7]

a mantra is a word, sentence, or prayer that is repeated throughout a meditation, either out loud or silently to oneself. The mantra is used in many meditative traditions, but the popular stereotype generally evokes the image of the meditator locked into the lotus posture, chanting "Hare Krishna" or "Om." This can seem silly, and the purpose of the practice completely eludes those who do not use it.

But in fact, the mantra is a powerful tool. In part, the mantra is a method of distraction, giving the wandering mind a place to focus in order to lock out extraneous thoughts. Or it serves to arouse deep-rooted, sleeping feelings of devotion to and reverence for God. In either case, the effects can be remarkable.

Some mantras are poetic, giving the very sound of the uttered words a harmonic glow and reminding the mind of an almost forgotten stillness deep within it. Other mantras are aimed at evoking spiritual ideals such as forgiveness, or synchronizing the mind with great spiritual teachers such as Jesus or Buddha. In any form, mantras help the meditator to let go of ego-centered awareness and open the mind to Spirit-centered awareness.

Many have discovered that when they use a mantra regularly, it can seem to take on a life of its own. Some people report that eventually their mantra practice becomes automatic. They no longer need to expend any effort repeating the mantra because it becomes a force all its own, like a heavy boulder rolling down a hill.

With this in mind, you might think that the mantra is some great, magical force that can transport you to enchanting lands or exalted states of being. Such things have been taught by many spiritual teachers, both great ones and, well, not so great ones. Yet here I must humbly and quietly disagree: No mantra, in itself, has power. However, when revered in the mind of the practitioner, a mantra can produce great results. The more you believe in a mantra's power, the more power it will have — for *you*.

For this reason, the mantra you choose should penetrate deeply into your heart. To begin, I recommend using a simple mantra that corresponds to your own spiritual background. Some mantras are better suited for Christians, for instance, than Buddhists, and some can be used by people of any faith. Choosing a mantra will require a bit of trial and error on your part. Below, and in tomorrow's discussion, I have listed a number of popular mantras. Which you choose is entirely up to you, but it is an important decision. Using the right mantra while you meditate naturally raises your level of awareness, while the wrong one might just irritate you. The words you choose should feel like powerful statements that work in your mind like medicine, lifting you further and deepening your awareness of your Spirit. As you repeat this word over and over, you become aware of the mantra and nothing else, and then you go even beyond it.

stop and practice

Twice today, morning and evening for about five minutes each, try one of the simple one-word mantras: *Om, amen, soft,* or *peace.*

1. When you are feeling relaxed, begin repeating your mantra at a calm pace, trying to focus your attention on the mantra and nothing else.

These short mantras are usually drawn out so that each repetition takes several seconds to complete: "a-a-a-o-o-o-m-m-m ... a-a-a-o-o-o-m-m-m," and so on. This may be done either out loud or silently, whichever you prefer.

2. Feel the word as if it were a powerful magnetic force. As it sinks deeply into your mind, allow it to draw away all of your extraneous thoughts and emotions. Listen to each sound of the word; imagine that the mantra is a living force and surrender to it all intruding thoughts.

3. When other words or thoughts intrude, make a firm, deliberate effort to recall the mantra to mind.

day 7

more mantras

*The ears were made, not for such trivial uses as men are wont
to suppose, but to hear celestial sounds. The eyes were not made
for such groveling uses as they are now put to and worn out by,
but to behold beauty now invisible. May we not see God?*

— Henry David Thoreau[8]

besides the mantras recommended for yesterday's practice, there are many others, each with its own unique effects. Don't worry about getting the pronunciations perfect! Few do, and it rarely matters, anyway. Just do your best with them. Some of the mantras used in the various meditative traditions are:

- *"Gate, Gate, Paragate, Parasamgate, Bodhi Svaha"* (pronounced GAH-TAY, GAH-TAY, PAH-RAH-GAH-TAY, PAH-RAH-SAHM-GAH-TAY, BOW-DEE SWAH-HAH). This Buddhist mantra translates "Beyond, Beyond, the Great Beyond, Beyond even that Beyond, to Thee Home." This is reflective of the feeling one gets as meditative practice deepens: that the meditations just get deeper and deeper with no apparent end possible. Just when you think you have touched the core of your spiritual Self, a deeper, more definitive experience opens up to you. Like the layers of an onion, layers of your identity are peeled back in meditation, each layer revealing a smaller version of the same ego-self until pure consciousness is at last reached. Sometimes in meditation you may feel as if you are shrinking, but only before opening into a much more expansive Self — "Beyond even that Beyond, to Thee Home." In fact, the entire spiritual path can be likened to a letting go of ever-smaller definitions of self in order to experience the core of inner being.

- *"Om Mani Padme Hum"* (pronounced AH-OWM MAH-NAY PAHD-MAY HOOM). Arguably the most popular Tibetan Buddhist mantra, this has various translations, each roughly meaning, "Om is a jewel in the lotus (flower)." Like the previous mantra, the sound of this phrase is a big part of its effectiveness.

The rhythm of the sentence is so perfect that it naturally draws the mind toward silence.

- *"Ram."* This is a Hindu word essentially meaning "God." Those with a particular affinity for the beauty of Sanskrit may find that this mantra suits them. Other names for God may also be used, such as "Our Father" or "Allah." The simplicity of these mantras, much like *Om* and *Amen,* can provide you with a very direct, easily recalled remembrance of your higher purpose. When you practice them deeply in meditation, you can recall these simple mantras any time during the day for quick relief from the grind of daily existence. As you practice, you begin to associate the word or words with the experience felt during your practicing. In this way, recalling the word helps to recall the experience.

- *"Thy Kingdom come, thy will be done."* This portion of the Lord's Prayer is one of many prayers that can be used as a mantra, either in part or in full. If there is a prayer from any faith that is particularly meaningful to you, try using a section of it.

In fact, virtually any phrase or word of devotion or prayer is suitable to use as a mantra.

The possibilities are endless. The only qualification is that it should be relatively simple for you to remember and should not arouse fear but rather lend itself to your own feelings of devotion.

If you find that mantra meditations work well for you, you will want to pick one and stick with it. Some people spend years practicing daily with the same mantra before they feel they have mastered it, while others never get much from the practice and should probably move along to other styles of meditation. Whether you are satisfied with mantras or struggle with them, trying out the practice can lead to many insights along the way.

stop and practice

Today try a different mantra than the one you used yesterday. You may choose from the above list or use one of your own. Practice it just as you did yesterday, for about five minutes two times during the day. Even though your technique will be the same as yesterday, every mantra is unique. See if you notice any differences in the state of mind each one produces.

day 8

the breath

One of the goals of spiritual practice
is to make conscious what was previously unconscious.

— Dan Millman[9]

talk to just about any yoga teacher and you'll discover that one of the first principles they teach is regulation of the breath. Most people tend to breathe too shallowly and irregularly, which negatively impacts both the physical and mental states. This is one of the reasons I recommended that you take at least a few deep breaths at the beginning of your meditation sessions.

Certainly deep and regular breathing is important, but in learning meditation there are far more important things to understand about the respiratory process. In our day-to-day activities, breathing occurs naturally, without our intent or particular awareness. We breathe without thinking much about it one way or another. In meditation, though, anything can become a distraction, including, strange as it sounds, a heightened awareness of the breathing process. As you meditate, you may notice that between breaths your thoughts are quieter, but as you inhale and exhale your attention is drawn to this bodily necessity, and thoughts suddenly invade your mind like a parade smashing its way down your block.

Like any other distraction, breathing in itself is not the real problem. Rather, breathing provides an excuse to be distracted. Our ego-self always seeks to disrupt any sense of peace that does not involve it directly. Allowing this disruption entails a willingness to let the mind be fully absorbed in its own constant clamor, often revolving around thoughts of bodily existence. And although it will eventually become clear to you that you are more than just a body, in the interim an acute awareness of the breath becomes the last remaining link to the physical.

But meditation is an ancient practice, and many before you have already recognized and addressed this problem. Practices dealing with breathing are among the most common forms of meditation. Some deal with concentrating the attention on a single physical point that the breath passes in its course, such as the nostrils or the back of the throat. During such practices, the practitioner maintains a focus on the chosen area, feeling the breath pass naturally back and forth but refusing to acknowledge its full course. This is much like any meditation that uses a single point as a focus — in this case, the point is the sensation of air passing a specific area.

Other methods use mantras to accompany each respiratory cycle; this helps keep the mind focused on the meditation instead of drifting into normal thought patterns. For instance, you could use a favorite one-word mantra both while inhaling and while exhaling, or you could say one word during the in-breath and a different word during the out-breath. Thus the mantra and the breath become synchronized, and breathing becomes part of the meditation, accentuating the silence between the exhalation and the inhalation.

These are only a couple of the techniques available for bringing the breath in line with meditation. By now, though, you should have some feel for my thoughts on the role of techniques. Techniques are valuable, but they aren't the magical potions some people make them out to be. You have to put them in perspective.

This brings me to a third technique for dealing with the breath: the simple recognition that *breathing is natural.* Breathing shouldn't be an obstacle to inner peace. The air we breathe is infused with vital oxygen, carrying life and renewal through our blood to our muscles and organs. A deep breath of air can be a thing of cleansing rejuvenation, relaxing our minds and bodies simultaneously. So during meditation, simply recognize that the breath instills harmony and is perfectly in sync with life, both in physical and metaphysical terms. Once you recognize this fully, the breath no longer feels like a distraction. This change in your outlook can make all the difference; the breath and Spirit are viewed not as separate, opposing forces but as operating in harmony, and so the mind grows still in the quiet beat of each rhythmic draw of air.

This recognition of the role of breathing is one expression of the view that all things work together in a mind that holds a single objective. This view describes the ultimate aim of meditation itself: harmony with life in whatever form you appear to be experiencing it. What better way to deal with any distraction than to acknowledge that rather than distracting you from harmony, it instead reinforces harmony?

stop and practice

Today, practice synchronizing your breath with a mantra. Once again, two meditations, each lasting about five minutes, should be sufficient.

1. First breathe in deeply through your nose, hold it for two or three seconds, and then exhale

through your mouth so that the out-breath takes about the same amount of time as the in-breath (for example, if inhaling takes you six seconds, then exhaling should also take you six seconds). Repeat this breathing cycle five more times before allowing your breathing to return to a relaxed, natural rhythm, now breathing only through your nose.

2. On your next in-breath think, "Breathing in brings peace to my body," and on the following out-breath think, "Breathing out brings peace to my mind." Continue mentally repeating this mantra with every respiratory cycle for the remainder of the five minutes.

day 9

attachments
---
holding on

If you do not make it empty,
how will you fill it up again?

— Neem Karoli Baba[10]

eachings on attachment have an important place in
many religious traditions. From the teachings of
Christianity to those of Buddhism, the general goal is to
love the Eternal above everything else, to purify one's life,
and to seek something more than the transient world before us. These great teachings all express one central insight: to have peace we must invest in what will bring us
peace. This means that first and foremost, we must recognize what peace is.

Some people seek money, others seek fame, and anywhere in between a million specific goals may bid for our
attention. But what is not obvious is that such goals
all have two things in common: first, they all represent

transient satisfactions, and second, everyone in the world at some point or another believes that reaching these goals will bring happiness. Let's break it down this way: people want money because they think it will make them happy; people want a new car because they think it will make them happy; people want fame because they think it will make them happy. And so it is with all worldly goals. We strive to reach them only because we believe they will fulfill us.

Personally, I don't think this striving is any great crime, but the real question that I would encourage you to consider is, Does it work? Does fame instill peace of mind? Can joy be purchased with wealth? More generally, my question for you is, *Where in all this big world can you find joy and satisfaction if you haven't brought it with you?*

This is not the sort of question anyone else can answer for you. Doing so requires that you become willing to objectively examine and evaluate your goals: Have they brought you true peace and satisfaction? Some people simply are not yet in a position to do this. And, indeed, doing so prematurely will only cause depression.

My own thoughts on the matter are really simple. I believe that worldly attachments do not bring lasting peace, but devotion to spiritual development does. But I also believe that before you make any big changes in your life, you should understand that although behavior may well reflect holiness, you cannot earn holiness through "good" behavior. It is impossible to reach God or enlightenment by simply abstaining from sex, or giving away all you own, or through any sacrifice or penance. What matters isn't the *physical* form of attachment — whether or not you own that fancy car or win that big case or have that great body. Rather, what matters is the desire for such things, the *psychological* attachment.

Let's take a moment here and be honest in our approach so that we can cut through a lot of the haziness that surrounds this issue. First, let's admit we are human, subject to mistakes, and that we are not, as things stand, 100 percent committed to the cause of our own peace. We still believe that some things in the world will bring us happiness, and we don't always embrace the presence of God, saying, "Your peace is all I want, Your presence is my highest aspiration, Your treasure is all I own!" Neither do we always embrace others in a way that reflects this commitment.

Recognizing these limitations is not that difficult for most of us; most people view themselves as imperfect creatures, uncertain, and at times even outright hostile. But we are far more than that! Try this on for size: You are a part of an Eternal Life, and just as it is impossible to earn holiness by altering your behavior alone, so it is also impossible to lose your holiness through "bad" behavior alone.

In other words, *holiness is an attribute of life*. You can neither gain nor lose your holiness through your actions. You can, however, remember it through your commitment.

This idea may be very hard to accept at first because we have been thoroughly conditioned to believe that behavior determines our worth. Since the earliest days of worship, humans have been drawn to the idea of sacrifice. For centuries people have sacrificed things of value: lambs, virgins, first-born children, and now, more commonly, all of the little wants and desires we deem inappropriate to the "sacred" life. In a sense we actually believe we can buy our way into Heaven.

The lesson I have learned and am still learning is that this doesn't work. I can't fake holiness, and I certainly can't "trick" God. As we do the real work of nurturing our spiritual life, in the end our desires and wants and consequently our behavior will change naturally. Behavior stems from thought. As you meditate more deeply, the goal of inner development becomes increasingly appealing, and so your desires will change. But this is a natural process. If you try to force changes you will more than likely end up feeling deprived, which breeds a distinct lack of peace.

So be open to change, but don't try to force it. Do whatever you normally do in your life, but give a little time each morning and evening to meditation, and above all else, develop a peaceful heart. Learning to live a simple, calm life based on kindness is the best way to learn the art of peace. It is far more effective than forcing chastity or sacrifice on yourself. Let your spiritual vision gain momentum first, and when you are ready the behavioral shift will be a happy one.

stop and practice

Try this focus sentence/mantra meditation twice today for about five minutes each time, and consider how it relates to the idea discussed today:

1. Inhale and think, "I act..."
2. Exhale and think, "...but I am not my actions."
3. Repeat this throughout your meditation.

day 10

attachments
using your desires

*Man's Desires are limited by his Perceptions;
none can desire what he has not perceived.*

— William Blake[II]

Yesterday we addressed the issue of attachments along the spiritual path and the idea that, for most people, sacrificing our desires may not be the best course to take. Today's meditation is an extension of this same idea. To really understand it, though, first we will need to take a closer look at the role desire plays in most people's lives.

Desire has a central role in human life. In fact, desire is the only force in all the world that shapes our lives. Nothing we do or think of doing is motivated by anything else. Even trivial decisions are enacted by the force of desire. For instance, changing the television station is done only because you have some desire to do so. You don't like what's on, or there is something else on that you'd rather watch, and so you pick up the remote and flip to a different program. Even those things that fall into the category of need still fit neatly under the banner of desire. When you *need* to use the restroom, for example, you also *want* to use the restroom, and every step you take to get there is motivated by your need-driven desire. Even when bad things happen that we don't want, our reactions to them are based on our desires. If your house caught fire you would most likely get up, and if you couldn't extinguish the blaze, you'd get out, call the fire department, and perhaps pray like never before! What if you were suicidal? Perhaps you would just sit around and wait to see what happened next. But in either case your actions would be based on your personal desires.

Look around your own world and survey your own actions. What motivates your behavior? In whatever we do, no matter how hidden or twisted the motivation, desire is the engine that drives our lives along. This holds true for both the pleasurable and the painful experiences each of us has.

Learning meditation, then, is really learning to redirect our desires. At first we learn to use tools such as mantras and visualization and breathing techniques — tools that focus our busy minds and check our busy thoughts. But what we really need to learn is to desire peace and spiritual illumination. Meditation tools are valuable only if we use them to kindle our desire for the type of deep peace possible during meditation. As you will learn, the deepest meditation is a silence and stillness that utilizes no words, prayers, or images. It comes from the power of an individual's undivided yearning for contact with their Spirit.

To achieve this contact, nothing at all is needed other than a willingness to let go of everything except a central focus on God. The peace that follows is only natural. So here is a new spin on what your desires can accomplish: you need do nothing but love God, love the Spirit, and let go of everything else, if only for a moment, and let your heart's desire open the door for you.

Years ago, I saw a picture of a yogi enveloped in a state of meditative ecstasy. The caption identified the state as "Samadhi," a Hindu term. This wasn't the sort of picture you would associate with the typical, serene meditative posture. Clearly this person was engulfed in a moment of extreme euphoria. His body was tense, and his eyes were rolled back beneath nearly closed eyelids. My impression was that he could barely contain the feeling.

Some years later I finally began to understand this state. I began to have meditations of the most intense ecstasy: my mind was filled with an indescribable joy, which, to be honest, felt a little bit like the sensation immediately preceding orgasm, except far more powerful, satisfying, and sustained. Previously, I couldn't have imagined the experience. Nothing I had ever heard about meditation could have prepared me for it. As far as I knew, meditation was nothing but a lot of work; it was something I did without really enjoying myself. I did it because I thought it was the right thing to do. I did it because I thought in the long run it would pay off, not because I thought it would bring me any sense of real joy. Boy, was I wrong!

In your practicing, then, attempt to let go of all other desires so that you can begin to open up to the deeper joy within. When you sit down to meditate, forget about work, school, money, sex, fears about the future, guilt over the past, and — most importantly — the negative emotions such as anger, jealousy, the desire for revenge, and so on. (Once again, I have to emphasize the immense value of forgiveness in overcoming these dark feelings, and in turn decreasing the resistance to meditation.) Release every want and need you ever had, or imagined you had, and commit yourself to that single, all-important desire for peace and stillness and the presence of God. Forget everything and everyone, and focus entirely on giving your mind over to your practice.

In this way you will evoke all the experiences and feelings that make meditation a joy rather than a chore. Once you are able to tap into these joy-filled states, meditation becomes self-motivating because you will *want* the feelings it brings. Do rich people need encouragement to enjoy their hard-earned and well-deserved wealth? Would a starving man sit before a feast in his honor and say, "Boy, this food sure looks great, but no thanks, I'll pass!"

When you learn that meditation brings real joy, you'll want it. This makes meditation easy. Then sitting down to practice will no longer be a duty, but the high point of your day. Then you won't need any discipline, nor will you need a mantra, or a mind picture, or any focus at all. Your one focus will be the peace you have found through your forgiveness-induced desire.

stop and practice

Before you meditate today, keep in mind that you want to ignite the fire of your desire and nothing else. One instant of heart-filled desire is enough to alter your perspective on life and God forever. This is the only purpose for today's meditation; put everything else out of your mind. Spend a couple of minutes considering how important today's practice is, and then give five minutes twice today to the effort.

Today we will use another mantra. This one is in four parts that synchronize with the breath (two with inhalations and two with exhalations):

1. On the first in-breath say (or think), "In this perfect moment..."
2. On the first out-breath say, "...dwells my perfect peace."
3. On the second in-breath say, "I cherish this perfect moment."
4. On the second out-breath say, "I cherish this perfect peace."

Repeat the four-step mantra until five minutes have elapsed. Try to get a real sense of letting go and opening to the type of desire that will do the work for you. Imagine that the words you are using are like a fire into which you are offering all of your extra thoughts and desires. Imagine that the words are working to purify your mind.

day 11

moving meditations
into the flow

Our physical body, the physical universe — anything and everything that we can perceive through our senses — is the transformation of the unmanifest, unknown, and invisible into the manifest, known, and visible.

— Deepak Chopra [12]

have you ever noticed the way figure skaters move in flow with their music? If you watch carefully, you will notice that the best skaters are those who just let go and focus completely on the present state of their body. It is as if they have entered into a tiny, spotlighted moment during which the audience and the rest of the world disappear and they are alone in the rink. In those brief minutes they seem to forget everything and everyone and let their skates sing in a way that echoes the graceful lines of Life itself.

Other top athletes must also exercise this same type of meditation in order to compete at the peak of their abilities. They may not call it meditation, but that's what it is. I have caught athletes, actors, politicians, police officers, doctors, talk-show hosts, psychologists, singers, and homeless veterans meditating without being aware of what they were doing. You also have probably meditated without realizing it. We have all experienced moments such as this from time to time. It's no big mystery. What I am suggesting now is that you consciously seek them out.

Meditation needn't be limited to the little amount of time you dedicate to it each morning and evening. You can find many moments during the day that allow you an opportunity to practice. These don't have to be closed-eye meditations. These "moving meditations" are important techniques that can help you transfer your meditation to ordinary moments.

You can consciously practice meditation during just about any activity. For instance, much of this book was written in a meditative state. You may even be able to spot some of the passages that I wrote from a more egocentric viewpoint, others written during very shallow meditations, and a few from still deeper states. These differences reflect my own shifting states of consciousness. The goal in meditative writing is to set your mind inward while allowing your thoughts to flow from the deeper part of the mind without clinging to the passing words and sentences, just as a figure skater may lose her self-awareness and tap into that other place in the human experience that, somehow, each of us remembers when we think of it.

Even something as simple as walking can form the focus for a meditation. In walking meditations, much as in writing, the mind is focused inward — something you will grow increasingly adept at — while letting your movements come naturally without attachment. You become intensely aware of each movement within every step — the motion of your steps, the rhythm of your breath, the swing of your arms. If this is done correctly, your movements become like prayers, quieting the mind and filling it with a sense of stillness and balance.

The overall aim of any moving meditation is transferring this sort of expansive experience to otherwise ordinary moments. Generally, meditation is performed with closed eyes, in stillness. Yet it does us little good if we are not able to maintain our peace during the course of the day. All of our time and activities can be devoted to spiritual development. It is really only a matter of motivation. As we realize the benefits of meditation, we begin to want to extend these benefits to every circumstance.

When we bring our meditative mindset to daily life, peace extends to our every step and breath, to our meals and our work, filling our days from morning till night. Folding the laundry can be a meditation; washing the dishes can be a meditation. In fact, all of our daily activities can be transformed into communion, opening us to the beauty of each step and every passing instant. Clarity is reflected in our eyes, actions, words, and thoughts, as a single devotion steps in to unite every separate aspect of our lives. In this way we can tap into the great internal flow and let our lives become a continuous meditation in motion.

stop and practice

Although so far you have been spending only a little time in each meditation, there is much to be said for longer sessions. For reasons that will be discussed later, it is important to gradually increase the amount of time you spend in meditation so that eventually each session lasts for at least a half an hour. So even if you don't feel completely ready, give ten minutes once today to the following walking meditation. You'll need some room to walk around a bit. Also, this exercise may look a little funny to others, so you may feel more comfortable doing it in private.

1. Stand up straight, facing an area that allows you at least ten feet or better to walk. Clasp your hands together and hold them against your chest.
2. Relax. Take a minute to let your thoughts settle down a little. Take a few deep, deliberate breaths.

3. While you are looking directly ahead of you, center your awareness on your body; become aware of it. This is the focus of today's meditation. Let every thought extraneous to a simple quiet awareness of your body and its movements drift in and out of your mind.

4. Very slowly and deliberately lift one foot up and forward, and then place it on the ground just in front of you. Focus on the movement of your foot. Up, forward, down. Once your foot is firmly on the ground, repeat the action with your other foot. Again, be aware of each slow movement of your foot and leg.

5. When you reach the end of your walking space, turn around using a similar meditative awareness of the action while you do it. Then continue your meditative walk back in the direction from which you just came.

You aren't going anywhere; you are simply meditating. Your focus is on the movement. This is really just like your sitting meditations in that as other thoughts intrude, you continually return to your focus.

day 12

moving meditations
movement and mantras

Your life is just a process unfolding.

— Ram Dass[13]

Some moving meditations have been specifically designed to bring the practitioner to deeper states through intentional, organized actions. Certain types of yoga, for example, use series of body postures, movements, and breathing techniques to arouse peace of mind through peace of body. Martial arts can also be a form of meditation; as in yoga, each gesture becomes a "letting go" that sows harmony between the body and mind. The thoughts grow quiet, and from this new perspective the practitioner loses the little self, the ego-self. Other disciplines such as Sufi dancing and tai chi also evoke a similar experience.

These traditional moving meditation techniques are rather complex, and so they are best learned directly from a teacher or through a video. Covering any of them in detail would require an entire book.

Another, simpler, moving meditation technique combines any simple, repetitive movement with a mantra, just as you learned to synchronize breathing with mantras. For example, you can combine a walking meditation with a mantra. In this exercise you not only focus on your movements but you also name each movement, either out loud or silently: "Lifting and placing; lifting and placing." Or, you can experiment with more complex mantra forms: "I lift my foot, which moves me ahead; I place my foot, which brings me stability." These particular sentences are reflective not only of the physical process of walking but of the spiritual path overall: Any change — whether it involves something as simple as walking or something as intangible as advancing on a spiritual path — brings a temporary sense of instability but is necessary if one is to progress.

Another variation is to use a favorite mantra in this exercise. Your mantra doesn't *have* to name your movements. Repeating the mantra "Om Mani Padme Hum" while washing a plate is a fine way to explore moving meditations, as long as it works for you. The point of combining the mantra with movement is to focus your attention on the activity at hand — the movement and the mantra. Each time your mind drifts to other thoughts, you recall it to your mantra and your movements. This is an extremely effective way to learn to incorporate your meditations into your daily routine.

stop and practice

Try incorporating a mantra with a walking meditation once today for about ten minutes.

1. As you did yesterday, stand up straight with your hands clasped together and held against your chest, take some deep breaths, and relax.
2. Lift one foot and say "Lifting moves me forward."
3. Set your foot down and say, "Setting brings me peace." Repeat with other foot.
4. When your mind drifts, recall it to your mantra and your walking.

day 13

extending peace

A man does not seek to see himself in running water,
but in still water. For only what is itself still
can impart stillness to others.

— Chuang-tse[14]

One of the main objectives of meditation is to learn to carry throughout your day the peace you find in your meditative practice. I discussed this idea in the sections on moving meditations. Again, meditation will do you little practical good if all of your efforts are abandoned the instant you open your eyes to deal with the day ahead. Most of your life is spent dealing with the world, and so if meditation is to be of any practical help you will need to apply it where it is needed. You can't escape from conflict by hiding from it or pretending it's not there, but you can learn to cultivate peace and bring it to the source and effects of conflict.

You are not the only one in need of peace. Just take a

look around you. Chaotic behavior and relationships exist throughout our society, regardless of race, gender, or socio-economic status. If you want to be able to improve the world and help others, you will have to do more than just talk about peace. You will actually have to live it!

Your responsibility to others is first your responsibility to yourself. A mind at peace naturally radiates healing. You don't have to make this happen; it happens of its own accord. Your only responsibility is to cultivate serenity — task enough — and carry it with you throughout your day.

Have you ever been around a person who is angry or agitated? Even though you were feeling fine just moments before, around this person you suddenly become tense. Our minds are extraordinarily powerful, far more so than most would believe, and we affect each other in ways that are never perfectly clear. One angry person can bring discordant feelings to a whole group. Mob mentalities are an extreme example of this. Another is when the "bad apple" at work spoils the entire workplace community.

Conversely, a mind at peace extends calm and healing to others. Have you ever known someone whose mere presence brings a sense of comfort to you? Naturally, we like being around such people. There's just something about them that eases our worries. These people have, to some degree and through some means, begun to come to peace with life. Such people are more rare than those who spread discord. The agitated agitate, and the peaceful bring peace.

Your practice of meditation puts you in a particularly favorable position to manifest this sort of silent healing expression. Each morning in your meditation, bring your mind to peace, breathe peace in as if it were oxygen, and learn to walk through the world with this same peace in your mind. Learn to offer it to those around you when they are suffering and angry simply by holding your peace dearly above all else. Be calm in the face of conflict, always, and truly challenge yourself to evolve spiritually.

Here are three techniques to help you learn to extend your peace throughout the day:

1. After you meditate, sit back and relax with your eyes open for two or three minutes. Enjoy the lingering quiet and try to externalize it. This may seem abstract at first, and so remember that using your imagination may help. This process is not make-believe, however. But allowing peace to flow from your mind and into the world can be grasped only by seeing that it does, in fact, work.

2. Pick a time in the middle of your day to close your eyes for a couple of minutes and try, however dimly, to recover some of what you experi-

enced during your morning meditation. This will allow you to experience the daily grind from a quieter standpoint, thus giving real meaning to your meditations by revealing how they can improve your everyday activities and relationships.

3. Craft some form of moving meditation from one of your regular, ordinarily meaningless chores, such as washing the dishes, doing laundry, taking a walk, or filing papers.

The effect of seeing your peace extend to others is profound. We are so used to believing only in what we see that we are apt to dismiss our meditations as selfish and ineffectual, perhaps even illusory. But if you are able to see that your own meditative practice touches others, the times you spend in meditation will take a sharp turn, becoming more relevant, more valuable, and more satisfying. Once you can provide tangible comfort to others without even speaking a word, meditation will become truly meaningful. You will have given the one gift the world truly needs right now, and it should be no great surprise that what you have offered to others, you will receive in return. Nothing in this world is more scarce than peace of mind; nothing, then, is more valuable to you, to those around you, and even to the entire world, than your ability to channel peace to others.

Think about it.

stop and practice

Today is the first of two "free" days in which I am not recommending any specific meditation. These days are intended to allow you time to explore meditations previously presented. You may choose to practice with the meditation you found the most interesting or with one that didn't seem to work well for you the first time. Whichever one you choose, read through the instructions once more to remind yourself of the essentials, and practice with it once today for ten minutes.

day 14

the guided meditation
inner journeys

The kingdom of God cometh not with observation;
Neither shall they say, Lo here! or, Lo there! for behold,
the kingdom of God is within you.

— Luke 17:20–21[15]

When possessed of an overactive imagination, the
meditation student can do one of two things: fight
it or use it. Naturally, I think you should use it. One way
to do this is with guided meditations, which are an elaborate kind of visualization exercise. They make use of the
imagination, guiding the meditator into contemplative
spaces through specific imagery. In a guided meditation,
you can embark on inner journeys to anywhere the guide
suggests; you can meet with anyone, whether they are
dead, distant, or imaginary. In your mind you can go to a
Buddhist temple nestled high in the mountains of Tibet,
reconnect with loved ones who have passed away and left
unfilled needs in your heart, offer forgiveness to people

who have hurt you in the past, or even sit down and meditate with Jesus.

Generally, you will need three things to practice:

1. *Imagination.* Most people have enough imagination to benefit from guided sessions.
2. *A guided meditation.* These are specific meditation exercises such as the one below. Each one offers a unique experience, so if one doesn't work for you, another might. If you would like to experiment further with this type of meditation, check with a specialty bookstore for literature on the subject.
3. *A reader.* Ask a friend or family member you feel comfortable with to read the meditation to you while you practice. (There are also ways to practice this without a reader; see Stop and Practice below.) But be aware that all readers are not equal. A good reader should be able to maintain a calm, even pace and a gentle tone, without too much stumbling over the words.

Some people think that much more happens in a guided meditation than meets the (inner) eye. Try it, and see what you think.

stop and practice

If you can't find someone to read the following guided meditation for you, there are a couple of other options: You can read through it and then reenact it in your mind, or you can record it on an audio tape and then play it back during your practicing. All italicized portions should be read. Do not read bracketed ([ ]) text, which provides instructions for readers. Additionally, ellipses (...) indicate a short pause of two or three seconds in the narrative, or until the specified action is complete (e.g., "Breathe in and hold it ... ").

Close your eyes and take a deep breath: inhale through your nose and hold it before you exhale through your mouth. ... Do this several times. ... Let your thoughts grow quiet as you feel a sense of deep peace settle across your mind. ... Feel your body relax with each breath; feel it growing lighter. Relax from your neck and shoulders ... your arms, hands, and fingertips. ... Breathe in and hold it ... and exhale through your mouth, feeling your legs, ankles, feet, and toes relax ... now growing even lighter and more relaxed. Take a few moments to let this feeling grow and encompass your whole body and mind, feeling as if you are sinking down beneath your thoughts into a very quiet and peaceful place [pause for fifteen seconds].

Now picture yourself walking amidst a beautiful garden, filled with trees and bright flowers. A brick path twists through the grounds, along a brook and up a rising green spread of lawn. The sky is spotless and the sun warm across your shoulders as you begin to walk up the hill. Silence marks the day, as quiet as the sky is clear, and an ineffable peace and stillness ease your mind.... This peace reflects the beauty of this place... reflects a growing silence within you... taking you deeper into itself.

At the top of the hill a small temple appears, with natural stone steps rising to wooden doors with black iron fittings. Pause for a moment and imagine that this temple is a holy place within your mind: a sanctuary set aside where you are always safe and perfectly at peace....

Walk up the steps, open the door, and step inside.

The lighting within is soft. The temple is perfectly empty and silent except for your footfalls as you walk. You see an inner door. Open it to reveal a stairway winding still deeper into the heart of the temple. You venture deeper into your mind to another door that opens to an inner chamber.

Before you enter, imagine that inside this chamber sits

a being of perfect holiness. Perhaps for you it is Krishna or Buddha, Jesus, Abraham, Muhammad, some other teacher, or just a great and shinning light. Decide now who awaits you inside [pause five seconds]*.*

Now enter the room and see this holy being sitting cross-legged on a floor cushion, eyes gently fixed on yours. Come closer and sit down on another cushion nearby. Notice that the hands of your teacher are soft, still, holy. The eyes are clear and shining with perfect compassion, which suddenly washes over you.

An aura of stillness encompasses the room, and a soft light seems to emanate from your teacher — touching your mind ever more deeply, quieting it and healing it. . . . The stillness is touching your heart now, quieting it and healing it as your teacher shares this peace with you. You can see a light shining from your teacher's eyes, and another shining from the heart, reaching out and shining into your mind and into your heart. Welcome this light into you. Join it. Allow yourself total surrender to it, as you feel it working within you to strengthen you.

Meditate with your teacher on this feeling of union for a little while. When you are done, stand up, give thanks to the seated figure, and exit the temple. Then open your eyes.

day 15

using music

*The song that we hear with our ears
is only the song that is sung in our hearts.*

— Ouida[16]

O f all the arts, music most closely expresses to me the intangible beauty of Spirit. In a way that is not clear, music arouses deep emotions and touches humans with a profound sort of magic that can inspire us to try the boundaries that limit us. Given this unique capacity for spiritual inspiration, it isn't surprising that teachers and practitioners have started to link meditation with music. Just as when broken-hearted lovers find comfort in music, so too can meditators find inspiration through the magic of music.

For the beginning student of meditation, music can be very helpful. During meditation, music serves the dual purpose of arousing devotion while muffling outside distractions such as blaring television sets and playing children. As with any temporary crutch, it is best not to rely on music entirely or for too long. Music during meditation may become a distraction in itself, obscuring the deeper experience of higher states. A related concern is that people who rely on music as an aid while meditating will become dependent on it, thereby imprisoning themselves in a fixed and limited view of meditation. On the other hand, if music helps you stick with your practice, it is better to use it than to quit meditating. Just keep in mind that eventually your meditations should reach the point where the silence itself becomes overwhelmingly appealing, and your focus increases so that exterior noises don't distract you as readily.

I used music during my meditations for several years and reaped tremendous benefits from the practice. In the end, the silence just beyond the sound was the music that attracted me most, and letting go of any attachment I had to this form of meditation was easy. As it turned out, the attachment I had formed wasn't to the music at all, but to something far more interesting.

Most people who listen to music during their meditations choose something soothing. Music designed to enhance meditation is featured on many different recordings, which can be purchased at any major record store. However, some people prefer to use music that was not written specifically for meditation but that is meaningful to them. You might choose music that you wouldn't ordinarily associate with meditation or serenity but that arouses heightened devotional states and drives you deeper into your practice (e.g., an especially beloved symphony, folk or popular music, etc.). What you choose is entirely up to you. I recommend that you start with something meaningful to you, avoiding music that stirs up fearful images or feelings of loss.

Musical taste and the particular emotions aroused by specific songs are intensely personal. Music can also be intensely powerful; the lyrics and the music can help to connect you to your meditation in a way that makes the time pass easily, when before each minute was a struggle.

stop and practice

When you are meditating to music, don't let yourself get caught up in the melody or lyrics. Instead try to focus entirely on letting go, as you would in any other meditation. Music acts much like a mantra in that, besides inciting devotion, another purpose behind the music is to distract the ego-mind. This doesn't mean, however, that the song should be the center of your meditation. Remember: you're not listening to music, you're meditating. Meditation means letting go. If you are able to get the balance just right, you may find that music is very helpful. Try it once today for ten minutes or so.

<u>day 16</u>

mindfulness

are you awake and aware?

The Past has flown away.
The coming month and year do not exist;
Ours only is the present's tiny point.

— Shabistari [17]

to be mindful is to be attentive. Mindfulness is the practice of being conscious of only one thing at a time without analyzing the experience. This practice can be applied to anything: a work or school project, reading, walking, eating and drinking, or socializing with friends. When you are mindful you are completely engaged in the activity while ignoring every other factor, whether it is something external such as a honking horn or something internal such as a stray thought. These things come into and leave your awareness without trapping your attention. In meditation, mindfulness may involve being aware of only one thought or one word, focusing on each breath or each passing instant. In this respect, mindfulness is an intrinsic part of meditation, which requires a focused awareness of one thing or practice to the exclusion of everything else.

To me, learning mindfulness involves learning a new awareness of time because mindfulness is a present-tense experience. In ordinary consciousness we are aware of the past, present, and future; the past is our memory, the present is our reality, and the future is our hopes and anticipations. Both the past and the future are only imagined states. We have no power within them. That is, we can't act in them or change them with any certainty. The present, then, is the only aspect of time in which we can change our lives.

In mindfulness, concern over the past and future is released, even if we are talking about only an instant gone by or yet to come. Mindfulness is a simple appreciation of the instant at hand. You become aware of your breath, of your movements, of the sounds and sights around you *at this instant.* You are not judging them in any way at all. You are simply existing in the instant and experiencing life directly. You are simply an awareness experiencing life around and within you. There is no force of will attempting to shape anything at all.

Mindfulness provides a way of learning to love every moment and, it follows, to love life in general. An awareness of the present awakens a strong sense of peace. There comes a love of life and of time, and a sharp appreciation for both the mind and the senses. Everything suddenly comes alive. You are fully present, and no single moment disappears unwitnessed or unappreciated. You are aware of your breath, of the sounds of traffic or a river flowing by or the rush of people heading for work. In large respect, you are aware of the very flow of life. More importantly, you are also aware of passing thoughts and the presence of your Mind that underlies them.

In this way life becomes a flow, a process whereby each instant is purified and exists of itself independent of the past or future. There are no worries in the practice of mindfulness because the future is not in mind — there is no judgment, no looking forward to anything and no dread or fear. Likewise, the past is gone and has no power to influence your appreciation of the moment. One moment is experienced and appreciated, as is the next, and the next, and so on. Each movement within your world, each sight and sound, join together, like different jobs in an assembly line working together to make a finished product. The mindful experience has a harmony and an assurance that no matter what may happen, no matter what has already happened, in this moment you are safe and at peace.

If all this still sounds a bit obscure to you, don't be too concerned. It isn't easy to communicate exactly what mindfulness is, or to learn what it is aside from trying it out. One thing is sure, though: when you do begin to understand mindfulness, it opens up the practice of meditation to an intense new level. So on to what's really important: practice, practice, practice!

stop and practice

Try minding your breath once today for ten minutes:

1. During your meditation, become aware of your breath. If need be, breathe in sharply and exhale sharply.
2. Now feel your breath as it enters through your nose and into your lungs. First be mindful as your chest expands, and then as the air rushes out. Feel this again. In and out.
3. Meditate on the sensation of your breath; be aware of it and nothing else. Don't think about it. Experience it. *Feel* it.
4. When you become distracted, breathe in sharply and exhale sharply, and once again return your focus to the breath. As in all mindfulness exercises, allow thoughts about the past and future to disappear. The instant at hand and the feeling of your breath should be your primary focus.

day 17

devotion
just let go

My dear child, you must believe in God
in spite of what the clergy tell you.

— Benjamin Jowett[18]

1 n every major religious tradition, mystics have come to similar conclusions when talking about the experience of being in God's presence. They say it is an experience of profound love. They say one cannot adequately describe the feeling. They say that it is both humbling and comforting, that there is an endless sense of peace and a fulfillment so rich that in comparison, all earthly success is like a raindrop to a storm. The power of love seems to be God's way of communicating with those who would open themselves to the divine presence. This presence, along with the feelings of love it brings, can be experienced and cherished and used for peace. We can let it shape our lives and

lead us along a way that heals us both as individuals and as a people. The mystics have said all this, and more.

Yet if we are to use love, we need to invest in love. We need to become more loving so that we will be able to receive the more powerful divine love. Without such preparation, the experience would be overwhelming, like sending 1,000 amps through a 20-amp fuse. We need to develop our capacity for love until we are completely open to it and can let it flow in and through us to others. In one sense, this is the entire spiritual path in short form: becoming an open circuit so that our lives absorb and reflect the peace of God . . . *and nothing else.*

Devotion is one of the great means for achieving this. *Devotion* means dedication. In devotion, you become dedicated to finding the love of God within you, or, more generically, you become dedicated to spiritual advancement. As your commitment matures, your ability to both give and receive love is vastly amplified. Suddenly you feel holy, you feel dedicated, you feel loving, you feel compassionate, and just as suddenly, your whole perspective shifts.

If the presence of God is one of love, then in order to experience this presence we must be committed to love. In our day-to-day lives, we need a sense that we are first and foremost creatures of loving compassion, gentle and kind before anything else. We need to begin to learn to love ourselves in order to accept the love of God.

These days, the word *love* is associated with weakness, whereas anger and aggression seem to be the motivating forces most associated with strength. For most people it's easier to be angry with someone than it is to embrace them and actually care for them. God forbid we should show some sympathy for a stranger, a tiny smile toward one who has hurt us, or reach down and lift up a brother or sister who is a stranger to us, yet a stranger in need.

At this point it may seem that such devotion *is* too difficult or too foreign to your way of thinking to make use of. Indeed, building devotion is a long-term commitment, a dedication. No one becomes perfectly devoted to anything overnight, and this is particularly true when we are talking about devotion to love or to God. But don't give up; experiences will come to support every step you take in this process, and so you will gradually grow convinced that as you embrace peace, you receive it. For now all you need to do is take one step in that direction.

So during your meditations today, imagine that you are a perfect, saintly devotee, committed to holiness, peace, and love. It doesn't matter if you feel dishonest in doing this. You are actually being more honest than you may realize. If you are able to succeed in believing this about yourself, even if it is only for a moment, you will instantly connect with the profound, divine love within you. This is a simple, yet effective, way to deepen your meditations.

stop and practice

Today's meditation is known as the Thousand-Petaled Lotus. As with all meditations, the primary objective is to keep your mind focused on the practice without letting it wander. Try it twice today for ten minutes each.

1. Pick a word with positive associations for you. It shouldn't be anything too personal. For instance, you might choose a word like *peace, soft,* or *devotion* (I recommend you use *devotion* for this practice since it corresponds to today's theme). This will serve as your focus word.

2. In your meditation, repeat the word silently to yourself and attempt to hold it in your mind for a few seconds.

3. Next, let the word be replaced by another word. This could be a word that is related to your focus word. For instance, if your focus word is *peace* you might then think *war.* Or maybe you will think of a word that doesn't seem directly connected to the focus word, such as *rain.* Just accept whatever word comes

to you, let it rise without your interference and consider it for a few seconds. Note its relation or lack of relation to your focus word.

4. Return your attention again to your focus word. Then allow another word to once again replace it.

5. Repeat these steps for the remainder of the ten minutes. You may find it difficult to recall your mind to your focus word without letting extra thoughts or words intrude. For example, you may think of the word *devotion,* and then *rain,* and then *thunder* and then finally think, "What the hell is the point of this meditation, anyway?" This is natural. When it happens, simply note what is occurring and return to your focus word.

day 18

paths
which way home?

Take the gentle path.
— George Herbert[19]

Some years ago I began rebuilding my life from the premise that life is a journey of learning. What I needed to learn was how to love more fully so that I could come to peace with others, myself, and God. In part this involved meditating regularly. As the years passed, though, too often I felt I was getting nowhere. I finally discovered — to my utter annoyance — that something was missing. I didn't want to admit it, I didn't like it, but the fact was I needed some help; specifically, I needed some guidelines, a path for the journey to a more peace-filled life. (Eventually I settled on *A Course in Miracles* as my specific path. See the *Recommended Reading* and *About the Author* sections for more details.)

One day, you too may feel you need some direction through life. If so, there are many paths to choose from. Some of these can be found within the major religions, such as Buddhism, Hinduism, Taoism, Islam, Christianity, and Judaism, while others are a little more removed from the mainstream. Each path has its ideologies and its quirks, its shortcomings and its strengths. From a broad perspective, they all appear to be distinct paths leading very different types of people to very different places. However, when you look more closely it becomes apparent that they all lead to the same place, and that even the sights along the way are much the same.

All genuine spiritual traditions share a number of similar guidelines, including prayer, forgiveness and compassion, right living and charity. Additionally, they all have two major factors in common: a goal and a way to achieve that goal, or a destination and a path to that destination. All spiritual paths offer guidelines for living your life in a way that will take you further along that path.

Whatever the specifics of your chosen path, the first step is to pause and understand that you are beginning a structured process through which you will change. The spiritual path is very much like a journey, and it will require effort, courage, determination, study, practice, patience, and understanding. There will be periods of confusion and pain, and quite a bit of struggle. You will have to challenge yourself. Further — and again, this is true whatever the specific path you choose — you will be given tools to help you along the way, elements common to all genuine spiritual traditions. In your devotion, these elements combine together to guide you to spiritual awakening.

Pause for a few minutes today and take some time to reinforce the idea that you are beginning a path of awakening. If you are already aware of your path, use the time to reaffirm your commitment to it. If you are just starting out, read through the following descriptions of some of the elements most conscious spiritual programs have in common and begin blending them into your daily life:

- *Reason.* Philosophy and contemplation are the bedrock of this aspect of the path. Reason involves coming to a clearer intellectual understanding of the specific spiritual path you are studying and, more than anything, understanding the application of its principles in daily life. Moreover, reason is also about honesty. Developing reason requires you to explore and discover the parts of your thinking that hold you back from spiritual progress.
- *Heart.* Developing your heart is developing your love for God and others, developing your

devotion and joy. It is emotion-based. Visualization meditations or exercises designed to open you up to forgiveness or devotion can be used to develop heart, as can prayer. As has already been made clear, it is important to learn to lead a life based on love, forgiveness, and compassion. This will automatically bring the experience of divine love into your awareness.

- *Practice.* In this book, the practice that is recommended is the sitting meditation, but every spiritual tradition encourages a variety of practices, such as prayer, worship, and the like. Whatever the specifics, the importance of practice is that it should always facilitate spiritual awareness.

- *Action.* As the saying goes, "To serve others is to serve God." In part, action involves the practitioner in meeting the physical and emotional needs of other people, thereby furthering the search for God. For instance, you might volunteer your time serving food at a homeless shelter, and through your care for others gain insight into God's care for you. The perfect example of this element of the spiritual path is the active giving of Mother Teresa and her followers. But action means more than just service. It can also be applied through the practice of moving meditations. Ultimately, action means letting *all* of your actions reflect your higher purpose; it is the outward component of your spiritual path that needs to be developed in conjunction with the others.

Beyond pointing out the need for these guides to the spiritual journey, I have no advice as to which specific path might be best for you. Whichever path you decide to embrace, keep in mind that the most helpful involve all four to some degree: reason, heart, practice, and action. Whatever the path, first we acknowledge that we are beginning a spiritual path. Then we take advantage of each of these four guides: we study the path until we are thoroughly familiar with its concepts, we embrace it and experience it emotionally, we practice daily, and finally we let it work in our daily lives to bring balance. Whether you choose to study Zen or Christianity is not as important as your ability to harmonize these aspects of the path.

What we ultimately need to understand is that any path to God is an internal experience. It doesn't take us from one physical space to the next, nor is it a journey across time. It is a process of purifying one's life at the level of thought and emotion so that resistance to spiritual awareness is minimized and we can at last open our minds to our deeper Self.

stop and practice

Today we are going to try another focus sentence (see Day 1). Even though spiritual paths and their corresponding beliefs are important, today's focus sentence serves to remind us that beliefs are not all-important. Your true Self is not your beliefs, even as it is not your thoughts, your actions, or your body. This is an important distinction that will be further discussed later in this book (see Day 30). For now, just use the sentence to focus your meditation, returning your attention to it whenever you feel yourself getting caught up in other thoughts. Meditate twice today, for about ten minutes each time, on this sentence: "I believe, but I am not my beliefs."

day 19

chakra meditations

If therefore thine eye be single,
thy whole body shall be full of light.

— Matthew 6:22[20]

oday's practice introduces another form of meditation, which for lack of a better description I have chosen to call "chakra meditations." Like all the forms we have tried, these require practice if they are to be fully understood. This may be even more true of chakra meditations than the others because chakras are difficult to understand from a purely intellectual standpoint. Nevertheless they are some of the most powerful meditations you can practice. There are different opinions as to *why* this so, yet the interesting point to me is that they are both highly effective and very simple.

The word *chakra* comes from Sanskrit and is used to describe certain key points along the body that are thought to correspond to what I call "spiritual hot spots" — places where spiritual energy is particularly strong. Chakras are a bit like the physical pressure points a martial artist might use to subdue an opponent. During meditation the goal is to focus on one of these chakras and, like a martial artist applying force to a pressure point, to activate that point through will. This focus stimulates spiritual awareness.

As with all meditations, the idea with a chakra meditation is to keep your mind on your practice while ignoring distractions. Instead of focusing on a word or an image, you focus on one of your chakras. For instance, one spot you can focus on is the so-called "third eye." It isn't actually a physical eye, but a subtler place within the mind. Its approximate physical location is a narrow point roughly between the eyebrows, set inward near the front of the brain (near the middle to frontal portion of the cerebrum). While meditating on this point, it is easiest if at first you do not try to find the exact spot, but instead direct your focus toward the broader target of your forehead. It might even help to imagine that you are actually staring at your forehead from inside your head. As usual, stray thoughts will distract you and there will be periods when you forget your focus and let your attention wander. Whenever this occurs, stop and redirect your attention, as usual, this time to your forehead. It's that simple.

Sometimes other forms of meditation are combined with the chakra meditation, just as the breath is sometimes used in conjunction with a mantra. There are many possibilities. You could, for example, focus on the third eye while repeating a mantra or while visualizing light illuminating it.

The third eye is only one point you might choose to focus on. Traditionally, there are thought to be a total of seven chakras. Besides the third eye, though, the only three I recommend for meditation are:

- The crown chakra, at the top of the head,
- the throat chakra, at the base of the throat, and
- the heart chakra, at the center of the chest (see the meditation for Day 4, for instance).

(For reference, the other three chakras are the spleen chakra, at the center of the abdomen, the solar plexus chakra, at the pit of the stomach, and the root chakra, at the perineum.) Each point produces a slightly different experience, and, as always, reactions vary among individual practitioners. If you choose to explore a number of these points, the most important thing is that you experiment only until you find one that works well for you, and then stick with it. In this type of meditation, as in so many, the longer you practice it, the more intimate you become with its subtleties.

stop and practice

1.   Imagine that there is a small ball of light (or, alternatively, a light bulb) shining in the very top of your head.

2.   Let all of your attention turn toward this light. Imagine that all of the energy radiating throughout your body is being drawn upward through your spine and into your head toward this light — as if it had a magnetic force — so that the crown of your head becomes your solitary focus, as if all of "you" existed only there.

3.   Maintain your attention on this light. Each time you realize you have forgotten about your meditation, return your attention to the top of your head. Try it twice today for ten minutes each.

day 20

contemplation
the thinker

Mirrors should think longer before they reflect.

— Jean Cocteau[21]

One of the beliefs I hold dear is that our thoughts, our faith, and our devotions hold tremendous sway over what we experience. Of all the great powers in the world, I think the power of the mind is the mightiest. Through the power of the mind our civilization developed as it is. Everything in our world that has been constructed by humans was built through our capacity to think and imagine, and everything in the world that was not constructed by humans can be used or appreciated only through the great power of our minds. We have a unique ability to communicate with and understand each other and to explore our lives and our environment. The power of our thoughts affects us in more ways than can be seen or imagined.

Contemplation, as it pertains to meditation, is an exercise in the power of mind. It is a deliberate exploration of life, philosophy, and beliefs, as well as, in some cases, a more direct contemplation of a physical object or sound. (For example, there is a form of meditation where an object — a rock, for instance — is meditated upon with open eyes.) One of the images that comes to mind when defining contemplation is that of Rodin's *The Thinker* — sitting with elbow to knee, fist to chin, and meditating on the mysteries of life, perhaps by the side of a brook or while stargazing during some warm summer's evening.

But contemplation needn't involve communing with nature. Studying spiritual literature or philosophy or pondering the nature of life itself — anywhere, whether by a brook or while stuck in traffic on the interstate — these are also forms of contemplation. If you believe contemplation only involves communing with nature, then I would suggest that a bathroom could work as well as a place for contemplation as a field or a mountaintop. The important part of contemplation is the deliberate consideration of an object or idea, not where it's done. Rivers, trees, and stars are lovely to look at. Just don't expect enlightenment to come from them. Comprehension, whether it is worldly or mystical, is experienced solely in the mind.

Our minds and thoughts are potent forces that shape

our lives and color everything we see. It is vital, then, to read, study, and contemplate the teachings that help us to shape our own thoughts into positive forces. Set some time aside regularly to read and reflect on spiritual teachings. Write down short quotes that inspire you and consider them often. In this way, through the wisdom of others, you will gain fresh insights into your own life and your own thinking process. Contemplation helps you to venture into the corners of your mind that are clogged with cobwebs, limiting your thinking, and it shows you ways to free yourself from them.

stop and practice

Try the following meditation twice today, for ten minutes each time:

1. Imagine that there is a "magnetic" light shining in your mind, right between your eyebrows.
2. Focus all of your attention on this light. Imagine that it is drawing all of your focus into itself, or that you are "pressing" your attention against your forehead.
3. Maintain this focus for the duration of your

meditation. When distractions cause you to forget about your focus, remember to return your concentration to your forehead. Each time you realize you've forgotten about your meditation, refocus.

day 21

the inner mind
a focus-point meditation

I do not require of you to form great and serious
considerations in your thinking.
I require of you only to look.

— Saint Teresa of Avila[22]

focus-point meditations are exactly the same as chakra meditations except that they deal with any point on the body, not just the chakras (see Day 19). Some points, such as the tip of the nose, the navel, the inner mind, or the length of the spine, are especially effective, but virtually any point in the body can be used during a focus-point meditation. As with chakra meditations, the focus point is chosen in advance, and the meditator then attempts to focus attention on that one spot.

Today's focus-point meditation is one that I discovered during the course of my own practice. I have found it to be among the very most effective meditations I have ever used, though why it is so effective is unclear. In teaching others to meditate, I usually recommend this meditation once the student has gained a little experience. Bear in mind, though, that unless you have already developed your ability to concentrate, this meditation may not be the best for you. In such a case, you should stick with something more concrete, like mantras or visualization. But don't jump the gun by judging your capabilities too soon. First, give it a try. If it doesn't work for you, allow yourself a couple more months of practicing other exercises, and then try it again.

stop and practice

As previously noted, it is important to develop the ability to sit in meditation for longer and longer periods of time, in part because sometimes it can take quite a bit of time just to settle down. During an hour-long meditation I have sometimes felt that for the first fifty minutes or so I was getting nowhere, but then, just when I thought all was lost, I went very deep during the last few minutes. So try increasing the amount of time you spend in meditation today to about fifteen minutes. This will afford you an extra five minutes for "getting settled." Meditate just once today to allow yourself to adjust to the time increase.

Do this focus-point meditation on the inner mind:

1. Try to get a feel for the approximate location of the center of your mind (as in the radial center of the brain), and then focus your attention on it. This may require a bit of imagination, as this image is a little more abstract than those we have tried thus far. But make the attempt anyway, and don't worry too much about success or failure.

2. Make this spot the focus of your meditation, recalling your attention to it when your thoughts go astray.

3. If you find it very difficult to focus on or even to locate the center of your mind, try imagining a figure in the shape of, say, Buddha or Christ, meditating inside your head. Gradually let this image sink into your mind until it is a small fixture somewhere deep inside, and then meditate on it. Imagine that it is leading you deeper into the center of your mind.

day 22

faith

The words in themselves are not important.
They are not the truth; they only point to it.

— Eckhart Tolle[23]

throughout this book I have emphasized the importance of experience in learning meditation. Today we are going to take a brief look at how experience also affects faith. There are two types of faith: blind and genuine. Examined at face value, both genuine faith and blind faith involve trust. A person with blind faith will trust that there is a Higher Intelligence without having any direct experience of the divine to validate that faith. Blind faith is the lens through which many people view their relationship with God. They worship, pray, and believe that they are being heard, that there really is a God, though they have no direct evidence. Still, their faith depends on _trust._

But faith can also take another route. We don't have to

merely "hope" that there is a God; we can actually experience God's presence within us. When our faith has developed through experience of the divine, it can grow from blind trust in God's existence into a genuine, experience-based trust that God will guide us throughout our lives, even when things around us seem to be falling apart. As Oprah Winfrey puts it, "I trust that no matter what happens, I will be all right."

Like forgiveness and meditation, this higher kind of faith can only be understood through experience. When we experience this genuine faith, we are aware of harmony with all of life. We accept life as it presents itself to us, and we let go of any attempt to control where life leads us. In such a state, we don't judge what happens as either "good" or "bad," but instead we rest within the certainty that both positive and negative experiences will pass and will ultimately serve to teach us the lessons we need to learn. Those who have genuine faith recognize that in the end, everything will work out for the best. They are on a journey of learning. This journey gradually becomes the whole purpose of life.

To help clarify the difference between blind faith and genuine faith, let me tell you a little story: Years ago I traveled down to southern California to visit some of my relatives who live in the area. While there, I happened to hear from a good friend of mine. I hadn't seen him in years, so

I paid him a visit. Since we had similar beliefs, he was excited to hear about some of the spiritual teachings I had recently encountered. Also present during our visit was a friend of his, someone I had never met before. In contrast to my friend's enthusiasm, this person did not like what I had to say at all. In fact he was practically seething by the time I left, and even though he never said a single word to counter any of my points, I could see that he held his tongue with effort.

The incident didn't disturb me, though. In fact, years later it sparked an amusing, though admittedly arrogant, image in my mind that helped me see that those of blind faith have the same problem as those of no faith. Picture yourself sitting by a pool, soaking up some rays and just enjoying your day. Along stumble two men sporting black blindfolds across their eyes and big, boisterous temperaments. You can hear that they are arguing over the existence of the very sun that is beating down on you. "There is too a sun!" bellows one. "No, there's not!" shouts the other. And so it goes — "Is too!" "Is not!" "Yes so!" "No, no!" — neither one able to argue convincingly what you know for certain. What would you say to them? "Fine, but could you move over, you're blocking my light"?

The debate both for and against the existence of a spiritual life beyond what the eyes can detect is utterly pointless. There is no need to argue. Everyone has the ability, with just a little effort and a little training, to learn to experience God's presence within themselves and to view their own true nature directly. This is how true faith is developed, through experience. So on to practicing!

stop and practice

Once today, allow fifteen minutes for exploring one of the meditations previously taught. As before, you might choose to practice with a meditation you found particularly engaging or with one that didn't seem to work well for you the first time. Whichever one you choose, read through the instructions once more to remind yourself of the essentials.

fear

hitting the wall

*And then, all of a sudden, Winnie-the-Pooh stopped again,
and licked the tip of his nose in a cooling manner, for he was
feeling more hot and anxious than ever in his life before.*

— A. A. Milne[24]

Y ou are scaling the face of a soaring mountain peak,
hard at work using every tool in your pack and every
skill in your résumé. The journey has taken you some
time, and over the years, through much work, your hands
have grown strong, calloused, and sure, and your mind is
focused on the task before you. Each movement of the
climb has become second nature. Steady and confident,
you move across dangerous, sheer faces, using for leverage
the tiniest fissures in the rock. The way, once difficult, has
grown easy under the power built through real dedication
and daily practice. There is joy in the climb. There is a
sense of unparalleled freedom. There is a growing silence
as you ascend higher and higher to a place where the air

and sounds grow thin. You are on your way, and the journey has become very real in a way you could not have imagined before you started.

But then, suddenly, like a shot of lightning from a sparkling clear sky, an overhang appears before you, arching back over your head to form an impassable block. You stop and look carefully for a way over it. Nothing you have learned thus far has prepared you for this task. You scan the rock for any tiny crack that can be exploited to overcome the obstacle. The rock, however, is as smooth as glass. You cast your eyes sidelong, searching for an alternate route, but you find nothing except more impossible obstacles. Next, you look down and see that what was commonplace on the way up has somehow grown into a monstrous maze, filled with hazards and offering no safe retreat.

As your predicament dawns on you, the world seems to drop away, your vision darkening as if you were in a point-of-view fainting scene in an old Hollywood melodrama. There is no way down, no way up, and no way around. As if for the first time, you realize that you are all alone. There is no 911 emergency line. No friends can hear your cries. Nobody in the world is in a position to understand what your problem is or how it can be solved. All you have are your skills, which seem to have all dried up, your determination, which is all but dead, and this confounded, impassive peak.

This image illustrates how fear can thwart your spiritual progress. For most people, fear is only a minor issue — the "anxiety" I addressed earlier. For those wishing to advance very far, however, fear can seem overwhelming.

Fear along the spiritual path is usually experienced as a fear of death, of insanity, of the world, of God, or of being swept away into the vast inner ocean of eternity. This stage of the journey has been called "the dark night of the soul," though not everyone agrees with this description. Whatever you choose to call this stage, it is a period of disorientation during which practitioners may suffer from a loss of identity and a terrible sense of meaninglessness; the things once loved are no longer appealing, yet the way ahead is still unclear or else appears to be too difficult.

If you encounter this obstacle, the first thing to keep in mind is that you are always perfectly safe. No matter how impossible the situation before you seems, remember that there is a resolution, and the fear will pass. It is not permanent. It isn't the end of the journey but, in one sense, only the beginning.

The second thing to understand is that meditation does not cause fear, even if this may seem to be the case at times. On the contrary, it helps to heal it. What is interpreted as the arousal of fear is really nothing more than the awareness of a fear that was *already present.*

Pain of any kind is merely a symptom that something

is amiss. If you sprain your ankle, the pain motivates you to take some weight off it. The pain serves a purpose. Pain is a symptom that can help a physician determine the cause and treatment of an illness; this is why the doctor will ask you not to medicate a sick child before you come in — medications mask the symptoms and make it harder to see what's wrong. Likewise, in spiritual healing all symptoms serve a purpose.

Fear is a symptom that motivates powerful changes at the level of thought. This is why I said that this stage can justifiably be thought of as the beginning of the journey. Finally the fear that has been with you all along becomes obvious, and you are motivated to make real changes in your life. The fear is a symptom like pain or a fever: When a sick child has no symptoms, nobody recognizes that there's a problem and so nothing is done about it. But when a sick child has a fever, it motivates the parents to take the child to see the doctor.

There is no need to approach meditation timidly or with trepidation; be confident that there is always a solution. In the end, fear is overcome through the total relinquishment of anger. If you do find yourself feeling trapped in fear, seek the help you need. In extreme cases, it might even be better to temporarily stop meditating. For those able to navigate this obstacle, however, an amazing surprise arises even as their fear eases: This terrible time is actually a great moment, because just beyond it lie the beginnings of real peace.

stop and practice

Because much of our fear is related to our physical well-being — sickness, death, and so on —it is important to begin to realize that we are more than just physical beings. Today you will practice a focus sentence meditation that addresses fears that stem from the belief that one's body and one's life are the same. The focus sentence is: "I have a body, but I am not my body." Use the sentence either as a mantra synchronized with your breath or as a simple meditation on the words. This time, though, try to keep your mind focused on a chakra or focus point of your choice. One fifteen-minute meditation is recommended.

day 24

the power of silence

The real in us is silent; the acquired is talkative.
— Kahlil Gibran [25]

from TV sets and radios to sirens, jet aircraft, horns, and the constant yammer of too many people with too much to say, our world is filled with noise. When we are not engaged in listening to something or someone, we are usually yapping away ourselves, either externally or at least in our own heads. As a result very few people have experienced true quiet. Imagine a silence that is so rich and reaches so deeply within your mind that it then expands to envelop the sights and sounds and people around you. This is a silence altogether alien to the workaday world and our lives in it. Yet this silence is something we can learn to experience and appreciate.

It is true that we can't make the world shut up, as much as we would sometimes like to slap a strip of duct tape across its magnificent mouth. This is one of the reasons I like to express my ideas via the written word; if you do not like what I am saying, you can always shut me up — just close the book. But even though we can't shut off the noise, we can learn to hear it differently.

By developing internal silence we are building a sheltered cove within ourselves, a place of stability from all the busyness that takes place around us. It is possible to see the world at peace when we are watching it through our own silent mind. This is the power of silence: the power to paint the entire world into a quiet place through the peace in our own mind. Remember, over our own minds we *do* have control. We cannot make the world shut up, but we can learn to be quiet and in turn to see that the world reflects our own hushed state of mind.

Right now it may seem impossible that you could ever experience this type of silence. But I ask you to consider that the nature of the mind is *naturally* one of silence. It takes energy to constantly think. Thinking is an action, something we *do*. Silence, on the other hand, is the state of the mind at rest, the mind unoccupied. So try thinking of it this way: silence is like sitting quietly, and thinking is like standing up and walking — only mentally. If you were on your feet all day, pacing the floor like a nervous father-to-be, wouldn't you be physically exhausted? Yet this is what we do in our minds all day, every day.

Practicing external silence is one way to broaden your understanding of silence and begin to see just how profound the amount of noise inside the mind really is. Sometime in the coming week, consider devoting a day, or at least a few hours, to silence. Go about your day as you normally would, except without talking. Observe the people around you without entering into the conversations. Watch your own mind, too, your own impulse to speak, and note any discomfort you feel with silence. In short, watch your thoughts. Are there any moments of quiet in your mind? If not, what would it be like if there were? Ask yourself what the great need to constantly think and talk is really about. Question the need.

This should be a day of contemplation, which always entails observation. Watch and listen, but don't engage. As a practical matter, you may want to carry a pen and pad with you for those moments when communication is necessary. Otherwise, simply pay attention to why and how people use talk to fill up their time.

Many people have devoted much of their lives to the practice of silence. Others regularly set aside a day for silence. I have heard that Gandhi, for instance, practiced a silent day once a week during his later years. For now, though, I am recommending that you give it a try just once. While it won't be the ultimate experience of silence — because, as you will notice, your mind won't stop just because your mouth has — the practice can be quite revealing, if not outright startling. It can help you to understand the incessant nature of your thoughts and see how they hamper your meditations.

After all is said and done, to be silent is to be at peace; a silent mind at peace is also a still mind, which is what meditation is all about. All we need to do in order to open up to spiritual awareness is be quiet and still for a little while. All we need is to stop talking and to be still in body *and* in mind, for which we really don't need to do anything at all. In fact, in order to experience deeper meditative states, we *must* do nothing at all. For just an instant we stop; there is no effort, there is no exercise, there is no meditation, there is no theology, there are no actions, there are no words. Through perfect silence and stillness, we experience an awareness of union beyond the body and the thoughts. This is the final and deepest meditation.

stop and practice

Practice "just listening" to the small spaces of silence in between your thoughts, making these silences the focus of today's fifteen-minute meditation. If it helps you, imagine that the silence beyond your thoughts is a powerful, living force that is trying to communicate with you. Let go of all fears, doubts, and restlessness today, and invite the silence to envelop you completely. Just be quiet and listen carefully.

day 25

a word on affirmations

*Tuning and training the mind as an athlete
tunes and trains his body is one of the primary aims
of all forms of meditation.*

— Lawrence LeShan [26]

having covered some pretty heavy theoretical concepts over the last few days, today let's turn our attention to something that is simpler and more concrete —
and is also one of my very favorite topics — words!

We have already learned how to use words as mantras
and as focus sentences, but our familiarity with them
makes them easy to use in many other ways as well. They
can inspire us to attain our highest goals and to seek out
our deepest capacities as human beings. Of course, the
words themselves are nothing, but the open-minded state
they can help us reach is vital to meditation.

An affirmation is a positive statement used to bring the
mind into a similarly positive state. Affirmations involve us

in a process of bringing *potential* states into *immediate* awareness. For instance, the statement "My still mind reflects only peace and holiness" may seem dishonest at first. Yet the entire reason for stating such an affirmation is to bring the mind to that state. A person who is already still has no need for such an affirmation. Those who are not at peace, however, begin from a negative state that must be curtailed. Positive affirmations are one way to do this.

Affirmations can be employed to achieve success in a variety of endeavors. Some people use them as a tool to succeed in business or to help personal relationships to develop. Some athletes use them to reach their highest physical potential, and affirmations can be a very powerful psychological tool for defeating minor bouts of depression, anxiety, and low self-esteem.

Our primary concern here, though, is to understand how we can use affirmations to aid us in our exploration of meditation, to "tune up" our minds so that they are operating on a level that reflects holiness. In one sense, we use spiritual affirmations to seek a state that already exists within us rather than one we are hoping to attain. The affirmations are reminding us of a reality that already exists, even if it is unrealized. Thus they are doubly effective: The goal of our practice is something real rather than something imagined. So the practice actually helps attune the mind to its natural, higher state.

Affirmations can range from very simple forms, such as a short sentence or even a single word that holds great personal meaning, to more elaborate versions consisting of multiple sentences. As you advance, I encourage you to experiment with many different affirmations, both during your meditations and throughout your day. These word tools can have a surprising positive impact on any facet of your life. And if your day is filled with the noise of thinking anyway, you may as well think positively.

Moreover, it isn't necessary to limit the application of affirmations to only one problem or another, or one time or another. Try to realize the power that simple words can have in your life when invested with faith and a truly heartfelt ambition. Also try to realize that in using affirmations during meditation you aren't being dishonest; you are actually affirming a state that already exists within.

stop and practice

"My still mind reflects only peace and holiness. Whether or not I am able to see it, peace and holiness are there. I want to experience them."

This statement contains three affirmations to be used in conjunction with a chakra or focus point. The first affirmation states a fact. It is true that your still mind does reflect peace and holiness, even though you may not yet be able to experience your mind as anything remotely still. The second affirmation takes things one more step: by way of positive reinforcement, it adds an additional fact, again one that may not be fully understood immediately. It reminds you that no matter how you currently view your mind, there is an unsullied state that can be experienced. Finally, the third affirmation fills in the rest, acknowledging that you desire such an experience.

So in this exercise, first you affirm your still mind's holiness, next you affirm that this still mind does in fact exist even if you are not currently aware of it, and lastly, you affirm your desire to experience it. Try meditating on this affirmation once today for fifteen minutes, working with it in much the same way as with a focus sentence. There is no need to repeat it like a mantra. Begin your practicing by saying the affirmation to yourself a couple of times, slowly, trying to absorb the full meaning. Then sit quietly while trying to maintain your concentration on the chakra or focus point you have chosen.

day 26

a word on prayer

For everything that lives is holy, life delights in life.
— William Blake[27]

m any years ago, when I worked as a public safety supervisor at a major Catholic university, I had a lesson in the simple power of prayer. It was early morning, perhaps four thirty or five o'clock, and I was going to the main campus chapel to unlock it before the morning mass. The sun had just begun to crack the night, and the new morning was silent and perfectly still. I had been up all night, and, as those who have ever spent a full night awake may understand, my mind was in a particularly open state — not quite a part of the awaking world but somehow still intensely absorbing the sensory experiences of the morning.

I walked across the campus to the chapel, happy that my night's work was nearly done and enjoying the last hour, when little needed to be done and things ticked along as a matter of routine. At the chapel I was unlocking the giant wooden doors in turn, opening each one to be certain they were fully unlocked, when I heard a faint murmur from within.

I peeked in: The chapel was dark except for the flicker of candlelight dancing along the walls. Curious, I stepped inside and looked around the corner.

Inside kneeled a priest absorbed in deep prayer. A dim row of candles lit his face, playing shadows across the high, arched ceiling and wooden pews. His stillness struck me, for it seemed to mirror the early morning outside. I stood and watched him for a few moments. I could hear him quietly reciting his prayer, though I couldn't make out exactly what he was saying. It didn't seem to matter. In those few moments a sense of living holiness washed over me, bringing me a moment's awareness of something deep within my own mind. In that instant the whole world seemed vibrant and holy, mirroring the priest's own intense focus.

As quietly as I had entered, I turned and left the chapel. I walked up to one of the nearby bluffs overlooking the sea of lights that comprise Los Angeles by night. There I sat watching the city below. The morning was still being born and so the day was still quiet and sluggish — really nothing at all had changed from the moment before

I had stepped into the chapel. Nothing outside of me had changed, that is. Within, I experienced a profound sense of peace, which, try as I might, I have never been able to accurately communicate. The experience was stamped on my mind like a permanent seal.

Prayer is another use for words that can be helpful during the practice of meditation. This is not prayer in the way we often think of it, which typically entails asking God, or the universe, for some *thing* — whether it is something physical, such as money, or the resolution of some specific problem. That morning in the chapel the priest didn't seem to be praying for anything in particular, but the effects of his prayer were far more revealing and valuable than any gift one could hope to receive on a material level. So to me, the power of prayer doesn't so much rest in the belief that prayer may produce effects in our physical circumstances as in its profound influence on the mind. Hence the deepest prayers ask for experiences of love, of God's presence, or of peace, as opposed to asking for a new set of headphones! This is not to say that we shouldn't pray for specific things, such as help in a real time of need, but in meditation prayer has another use.

Use prayer as a tool, much like a mantra or an affirmation. *Feel* the prayer rather than repeating it blindly. Let the prayer work to open your heart to devotion, and unlock your mind to the deeper presence of your Soul. You may find, as I have, that through prayer you become capable of much deeper meditations than you believed possible. You may also come to see how your own sense of holiness can spread naturally to other people, just as the priest's prayer had such a dramatic effect on me.

stop and practice

Use prayer at the beginning, middle, and end of your meditations today, using whatever form of prayer you prefer. Keep in mind that meditative prayer is a type of asking — not for some thing or some change in circumstances but for an experience, a state of being. In the bigger picture, experiencing a higher awareness helps us solve all of our problems. When we are able to open our minds to God, to all the love that pours forth from the Heaven within us, then all of our problems are seen in a new perspective. Even if they are not solved outright, at least our minds are clear and we learn to see them in a context that promotes growth.

Two fifteen-minute meditations are recommended for today. If you don't have a specific prayer in mind, try the following one or some variation of it to suit your preferences:

Our Father (or Holy Mother, Dear God, Allah, Great Spirit, Lord, et cetera),

Let me come into Your presence now; fill my mind with Your peace and Your joy. Let all my thoughts be as Your thoughts are; let my will be as Your will is. In this moment, I offer myself to You, to guide me along the way back to You. Amen.

day 27

on healing

A little with quiet is the only diet.

— Scottish proverb[28]

i have been sitting here in front of my computer, strain-
ing my brain to think up some witty, impressive, or
just plain entertaining way to introduce the subject of
healing. But the fact is, I don't think my attempts to
lighten the subject would be much appreciated by sick
people looking for help, perhaps desperately. So forgive me
for this clumsy introduction. This is a touchy subject, and
many books have already been filled with words about it.
To keep within our focus on meditation and to avoid
going beyond my own experience, then, I will be brief and
straight to the point.

The very first thing to keep in mind when attempting
to use meditation as a tool in dealing with illness is that if

you need to see a doctor, then you should. If you are sick with an illness that requires the services of a physician, don't try to rely on meditation as a substitute. The best treatment plan is to select your doctor carefully, research the illness and its treatments, and use meditation only to supplement those treatments.

Every once in awhile there is a story in the news about a child with a treatable disease who has died because the parents let the disease go untreated "for the sake of faith." There is no cause for such painful lessons, and I bid you to learn from these mistakes. If you need help, go get it! This is also true of mental disorders as well.

That said, meditation can be a powerful aid to healing, and the specific technique I recommend is visualization. The images do nothing in themselves; the primary function of visualization as it pertains to physical healing is to stimulate the mind's ability to aid recovery. Medical science, now more than ever, is recognizing the mind's ability to influence physical well-being. In visualization, the idea is to imagine real healing in conjunction with the prescribed medical treatments. For instance, someone who is undergoing radiation treatment for cancer might visualize the radiation — both during and after the treatments — as a soft white light penetrating the body, dissolving the cancer while leaving the healthy tissue untouched. Or someone who is taking antibiotics to treat a bacterial infection might imagine the medicine flooding their bloodstream and into the area of the infection, where it aggressively works to dissipate the bacteria.

Whatever the circumstances, the best way to use meditation for healing is to stay in the moment, to stay with the image. Let your mind grow completely quiet and focused on the image, and forget about everything else. Forget about the potential consequences if your treatment doesn't work. Use the time in meditation, which should last at least twenty minutes each day during the course of treatment, to put aside all anxieties about your future. Let go of every thought but the image you have chosen to represent healing in the present moment. Using visualization as an aid to healing is just as simple as that.

There is one more point to understand, though: Seeking only long-term health is a no-win proposition, and constant health should not be an end-all goal of meditation. Why? Because eventually everyone's health will fail. Thus, our comfort and security must rest in the awareness that we are more than just physical creatures with finite lives.

Along the way, it is natural to seek health and avoid illness, and as a practicality we can use our meditation to promote both health and healing. Whether this involves actually calling down some Great Power from Heaven or something a touch more mundane such as using the power of our beliefs, visualization can aid us in harnessing our will to heal, helping us to focus and rise above every earthly circumstance. In the end it is the experience we find within our own minds that gives our transitory existence purpose and joy.

We can come to peace with aging and sickness, and we can learn to keep our minds on the presence within us that will never grow sick and die. This is the greatest goal. Don't ever lose sight of it, whatever you do or experience, through both sickness and health. Then everything you go through will have meaning, and there will always be hope in your life, no matter what comes your way.

stop and practice

Try this exercise twice today for fifteen minutes each time. If you are suffering from an illness or desire some specific healing, focus the images in the exercise on your own situation.

1. Imagine the air around you infused with a sparkling, soft light, subtly glowing as if it were alive. See the light resting on your body, on your arms and legs, chest and stomach, and gently caressing your eyelids and face.

2. Now, as you inhale, imagine the light entering your nose and spilling into your lungs. Then, as you exhale, imagine it radiating into and throughout your body. Try to imagine this as vividly as you can. Let your mind become fully engaged with this fantasy. This is your focus for today.

3. Finally, imagine that the light is all around and within you. Pause for a moment and sense the boundaries between you and the light begin to dissolve, so you are becoming a part of the light, and it is becoming part of you. Sense that this light is imparting healing to you, strengthening your body and bringing peace to your mind.

day 28

beyond form

Face to face he beholds the unbroken Truth, the Truth beyond all truths, the formless Origin of origins, the Void which is the All; is absorbed into it and from it emerges reborn.

— Eugen Herrigel [29]

beyond all the practices we have tried so far, there is another type of meditation that relies on no specific practice at all. It involves no mantras and no contemplations, there are no specific visual images to focus upon, no focal point to recall your attention to. Instead there is "just sitting" — letting thoughts come and go and experiencing the moment and life exactly as it is.

It has been said that this type of practicing, which is often called "formless meditation" — meditation beyond words, images, instructions — is the purest form. It recognizes that all specific practices at best only lead one to pure consciousness, like a boat transporting its passengers to an island. The boat itself is just a vehicle, not the destination, and it must be abandoned eventually if one is to be truly free. In formless meditation the focus of the meditation becomes the meditative awareness itself. In this state, words are of no use. Either you understand it or you don't.

Formless meditation evokes a total, direct awareness of a formless, unattached Life that lies beyond everything we can see and hear and touch, beyond both time and space. Dwelling in this Life requires us to become free awareness, or perfectly aware, which means that we are perfectly free from all judgments. In this awareness there is no distinction between "good" and "bad," "north" and "south," "black" and "white," "rich" and "poor," "up" and "down," "seconds" and "years," "life" and "death," "meditation" and "non-meditation." Everything, including the mind, is experienced directly, as it is, with no adjustments, no seeking, no resistance.

In this state of free awareness, every instant is the same as both the last instant and the next, so that there is nothing but one eternal reference point. There are no thoughts of what has gone by or what is yet to come. We are aware only of the present moment: the passing sensations, sounds, and smells experienced in each instant; we hear the rain falling outside, the hum of traffic and computers, and we experience the feeling of sunlight or darkness pressing against our closed eyes. There is no hatred or fear or love or joy. There is only a life, like that of a tree that neither retreats from the ax nor revels in light, a life that does not question and wonder, do this or that, say "What am I, and what is my purpose today?"

This is the highest awareness, the state that all forms of meditation are meant to lead to. It is quite simple; formless meditation is merely a meditation on the experience of unity with Life. Yet there is no way to intentionally practice it or seek it out. It is not a doing. It comes when we are open to it, and when we resist, it can't be found. This pure awareness knows the Everything beyond all form, and as such it does not require any amount of time or study or practice to reach. All that it requires is our unflinchingly open mind. We let go of everything in order to experience Everything.

stop and practice

Practice "just sitting" today, relying on no particular focus at all. Let all your thoughts just come and go. Maybe you'll note, "Now I am thinking of this and letting this thought go, and now I am thinking of that and letting it go," but keep in mind that even this recognition is like the other thoughts that pass through your mind. Whenever you think of the past, of rights or wrongs, anticipations over future states and experiences, even when you think of God or meditation, simply let these thoughts disappear. Try to experience this perfect state of "just being" for a little while today, all the while knowing that even this attempt is a doing. True not-doing is an awareness. In it there is no attempt at all. Such is the paradox of practicing "non-practice."

character traits
practice what you preach

Patience and passage of time
do more than strength and fury.

— Jean de La Fontaine[30]

W hen we first start along a spiritual path, it is certain that we harbor views that are not helpful to the journey, no matter how advanced we believe we are. Meditation gently loosens your grip on these fixed views, opening your mind to new ideas that previously remained unconsidered or even intentionally ignored. Some of the insistence on clinging to old beliefs and values has to do with a fear of change. But more than anything, it has to do with fearing a loss of identity. When you accept any idea into your mind and cherish it, you actually see this idea as a vital part of your existence, so much so that you may seek to defend your ideas at the cost of your own peace of mind.

Many people seek out conflict, even unconsciously. As you develop through meditation, though, you get a taste for living without conflict, even if it is only within the narrow periods of your actual practice. These brief experiences of peace create the motivation for major life change — the change from a state of conflict to a state of peace.

The contrast your practice reveals between the peace of meditation and turmoil of conflict makes clear that any attraction to pain and discord are psychological states, and as such are dependent on faulty human thought processes. This, in turn, leads to the development of certain positive characteristics, which are worth considering and eventually cultivating. The practice of meditation both lends itself to these traits and is also deepened by their manifestation. Some of these traits are patience, compassion, simplicity, and gratitude:

- *Patience.* Developing patience requires the recognition that you have little control over other people. For instance, on your way to work, you may be annoyed that some people drive too slowly and others too fast, at least in your view. But either way you are not able to change their behavior substantially. So your annoyance has no power; it does nothing except disrupt your own peace. When you accept the fact that you cannot control other people, you are then free to choose whether or not your own peace is worth tossing away because other people refuse to meet your standards.

You'll get to work either way. What you will choose is really the state of mind you will be in when you arrive. Will you be frazzled and annoyed, or will you be calm, quiet, and ready to begin the day positively? You cannot control or predict life. So just let it be. This is the justification for patience.

- *Compassion.* Compassion is far more than feeling sorry for someone. It is a powerful force that frees your ability to care for yourself by caring for others. Through compassion, you learn not to attack; where attack seems due, you instead realize that people who attack you are in desperate pain themselves. What they really need is your forgiveness and compassion. This will help both you and them.

- *Simplicity.* It makes sense that those who desire peace recognize the value of living a simple life. Elaborate desires and needs add unnecessary complications to our lives. Of course, how complex you make your life is entirely up to you, but at some point, through meditation, you may perceive a web being woven around you by the intricacies of false needs. When this web becomes apparent, you will naturally see the value of simplicity and seek it out.

- *Gratitude.* This one is simple. A mind at peace is full of gratitude. A peaceful mind is grateful that it has found a better way to live. It is grateful for the awareness of being an eternal part of an Eternal Life. A peaceful mind learns to love its own thankfulness and seeks to share it, all in the name of gratitude for God and for others in the world. A peaceful mind sees beauty within and without. This gratitude is largely the result of living a simple life filled with compassion and patience. Open your heart to gratitude and you will naturally understand each of the other traits with no effort at all.

Make it a point each day this week to work on developing these four traits. Select one trait to focus on today, one to focus on tomorrow, and so on until you at last feel their pull begin to transform your life. Like forgiveness, they are great motivators; once they are practiced with sincerity they have the power to transform lives overnight and to increase the power of your meditations in a single, sincere instant.

stop and practice

Practice this meditation on gratitude two times today for fifteen minutes each time:

1. Imagine some of the people in your life: friends, family, coworkers, acquaintances, neighbors, enemies — whoever occurs to you.
2. Picture them standing with you, hand in hand, in a circle.
3. Carefully consider the person standing next to you. Say to this person, "Thank you for playing a part in my life. I wish you peace and happiness in your life." Then move on to the next person in the circle.
4. Repeat this exercise throughout both your meditations today. If you run out of people to work with, finish your meditation using whichever technique you would like.

day 30

the power of choice

*The club that kills can drive a stake
into the ground to hold a shelter.*

— Gary Zukav[31]

oday's idea is simply that to empower your life, you have
to seize responsibility for it and then apply the conscious
force of your determination to change it. Peace with God
and life can only arise through your desire for it, which will
automatically direct your will. You cannot wait and hope
that God or yet another "miracle pill" will somehow solve
the problems of pain, dissatisfaction, and depression that so
many people experience. If you are not at peace, you will
not change your state by doing nothing about it or by blam-
ing other people for your pain. Although this seems obvious, it is a lesson very few have fully grasped.

In the discussion on forgiveness on Day 3, I demon-
strated how the laws of forgiveness operate like physical

laws by using Newton's third law of motion: "every action has an equal and opposite reaction." Another of Newton's laws of motion is that "an object at rest tends to stay at rest, while an object in motion tends to stay in motion." This, his first law of motion, also holds that this rest or motion will continue unless the object is acted upon by another force. In simple terms this means that if a runaway train is rolling downhill, it will not stop unless the breaks are applied or some other force intervenes. In space, where there is no friction to pose any resistance, a moving object could theoretically stay in motion forever. Similarly, an object that is not moving will require a "push" to set it in motion. A car needs an engine to move forward. Without one, it won't budge.

This law is essentially stating the obvious: nothing comes from nothing. This is true in spiritual development as well. If you want something to change in your life, you will need some force to get things moving or to shift direction. A mind in conflict will tend to remain in conflict unless it is acted upon by a force capable of producing some change.

This book has been about more than just meditation. It is also an introduction to another way of living life, one that involves seizing responsibility for your own well-being and choosing peace instead of conflict. Empowering your life begins by admitting what and who you are — in all terms, good and bad — and then recognizing that you have gotten to this moment in your life through your choices, and that you can move in a new direction by choosing differently. You have this greatest of all powers. You can change your life, or not, simply by the living force of your desire.

Moreover, it is important to realize that your choice is really between only two distinct paths: you can walk the path of love, with forgiveness and compassion as your guides, or you can walk the path of judgment, with fear and anger by your side. Furthermore, whether you realize it or not, you do choose between these two paths *every day.* You cannot be in the world without walking one path or the other. Neither is there a way to seek an alternative beyond these two; you are on one of these two paths right now, at this very instant; and so am I. Now each of us needs to ask ourselves, How do I feel? Which path have I chosen? And we need to realize that if we are unhappy with our choice, there is an alternative.

Recognizing this alternative is really where everyone who has sought and found change for the better has started: an honest evaluation followed by an intelligent course of redemption. Sometimes it takes horrendous suffering for people to really reconsider the way they have been living and to ask if a better way might be possible. One of the terrible tragedies of being human is that we tend to be so short-sighted that we sometimes forsake our own good in favor of doing things "our own way."

So each day stop briefly and reflect on your state of mind, and realize that you have the responsibility and the power to choose your path. Each morning ask yourself which path you would like to walk during the day ahead, and then consciously seek it. And whenever you are sad or angry or afraid, remember that you have made a choice to walk this path and that if you are unhappy you can always choose differently. Even when negative circumstances are thrust on you, you still must select how you will view them. When other people are hateful toward you, you still do choose how you will react to and view them. Instead of becoming defensive and angry in return, it is equally easy to realize that angry people are unhappy with themselves, and so what they really need is kindness.

And don't for a moment believe that this is some silly, naïve, utopian idea that will never work in the real world. Use your free will to employ this way of living and you will see not only that it works but also that it gives you a position of power unmatched in all the world. What you are really choosing is your underlying attitude toward life, which affects everything you see, hear, and do. It is the power of choice that directs both "the club that kills" and the one that "drive[s] a stake into the ground to hold a shelter." Which will you choose?

stop and practice

Today we are going to bring together the four focus sentences you worked with previously, adding a new element. This meditation is actually a variation of a Hindu practice known as the "Who am I?" meditation. In one sense it is a contemplation meditation, yet the question posed cannot be answered in words. By posing the question "Who am I?" you are really seeking an experience of the Self as an answer.

1. Begin your meditation by asking, "Who am I?" Then remind yourself of the focus sentences: "I think, but I am not my thoughts. I act, but I am not my actions. I believe, but I am not my beliefs. I have a body, but I am not my body. Who, then, am I?"

2. Answers will occur to you naturally. For example, you might think, "I am my name," or "I am American," or "I am a spiritual being," or an astronaut, a banker, a lover, human, a strong person, or the like. Whatever comes to mind, remind yourself that this is not "who you are" but just an image or a role that has

been added onto the essence of your Self. If you think, "I am male" or "I am female," "I am healthy" or "I am ill," remind yourself "I have a body, but I am not my body." If you think, "I am smart" or "I am dull," remind yourself "I think, but I am not my thoughts," and if you think "I am my occupation," answer "I act, but I am not my actions." In this manner let every image of yourself be answered with one or more of the focus sentences.

3. When nothing occurs to you, repeat the focus sentences one by one, along with the question "Who am I?" to recall your attention to the question. Remember, you are really seeking a pure experience of who you are, which is not something for words to answer.

part 3

the journey

continues

bits and pieces

external learning

A good book is the precious life-blood of a master spirit,
embalmed and treasured up on purpose to a life beyond life.

— John Milton[1]

t he practice of meditation is like a puzzle: bits and pieces of it will remain a mystery until the whole picture is completed, and only then will things become clearer. There are certain elements to the practice we simply cannot uncover through words but instead must discover through our individual practice, our internal learning.

Still, the development of our ideas is a part of the puzzle, and few people can begin to organize their minds without some initial guidance, some external learning. We are far too focused on the world and trapped within our beliefs to simply let go of our judgments with no guidance. So how should you proceed from here? I cannot give you all the answers, but I can fill in some missing pieces.

With this in mind, this section covers the elements of the spiritual path that relate to external learning, such as religious traditions, meditation groups and teachers, retreats, and books. Each person reacts differently to these various types of guidance, and so it must be up to you to choose a way that suits your personality and needs. Which is right for you? You may have to do some exploring to find out, and in the end this exploring can be as helpful as dedication to the path you finally settle on.

world religions

Most of the major religious traditions include meditation in their practice, though they may not use the word *meditation* to describe it. Buddhism and Hinduism are obvious examples, and so if your background, interests, or temperament attract you to one of these traditions, you should have no trouble finding the necessary guidance you will need. But few realize that Christianity, Islam, and Judaism, with their rich mystical traditions, lend themselves very nicely to meditation. As noted early on in this book, you need not change your religion to meditate. Other people may place limitations on what may be practiced within the confines of your particular religious tradition, but don't accept other's conclusions about whether or not meditation is right for you in conjunction with your beliefs. Meditation goes well with any love-based theology, provided you are given the freedom to explore and develop your beliefs.

If you are interested in how your own religion views meditation, you can do one of two things: First — and I know this sounds extreme —you could try simply asking. Call local places of worship and check with their clergy; search the Internet, combining the word "meditation" with whichever tradition you're interested in; or — another quaint idea — inquire with your local librarian, who should be able to steer you in the right direction.

meditation groups

The word *cult* comes from the Latin *cultus,* or adoration, and in the broad sense it refers to any body of religious beliefs and practices — even the most traditional. Yet to the average person, the word is loaded. In its more familiar meaning, the word *cult* means religious worship that is new, unorthodox, or just plain weird. Though not inherently negative, the word *cult* is increasingly associated with dangerous beliefs (think Jonestown and Waco, Texas).

Besides the major world religions, smaller spiritual movements are afoot all across the globe today, and many of these have incorporated various meditative practices into their traditions. Some of these might indeed be considered cults, in the weird sense. But these days any small spiritual group is stamped with the word, and it can be impossible to tell for sure. Given all this, your first question when considering whether or not to get involved in a meditation group might very well be, "Is this group a cult?"

But before we go any further, here is a fact to consider: Scandals have arisen from time to time even in the largest, most well-established religions. Think of all that has occurred lately in the Catholic Church. Moreover, such scandals are just the tip of the iceberg, the big messes that showed up on the radar, so to speak. Take a close-up shot of religion in general and you'll find many cases of abuse, strange beliefs (religious beliefs are all strange except to those who hold them), and supposedly loving environments that in fact teach intolerance, fear, and other damaging views. So here I would suggest that rather than asking whether any particular group is a cult, you might be better off asking, "Is this group dangerous or simply not helpful?"

There is plenty of craziness in the world. In fact, there's enough of it to be shared equally by both the major religions and the "cults" alike. The bottom line is, you certainly needn't be afraid to explore smaller spiritual organizations as long as you exercise intelligence and basic caution in doing so. I would suggest that you use the same caution when evaluating any established religion as well.

Keep these things in mind as you begin to incorporate the practice of meditation into your life. There may come a time when you will want to seek out other like-minded individuals to share your journey. At some point you may find that your emerging understanding of God will call on you to reconcile your long-held beliefs to new experiences. As a result, old systems of theology may not satisfy you as they once did, and popular religious views may become too limited in scope. As always, be open to change. If your old place of worship suddenly begins to feel unenlightened, stagnating, or somehow unfulfilling, by all means move along — or at least find an additional source of support that better fits your new experiences. Life is now becoming a journey, and like all journeys some change is involved.

For those who are not interested in what the major religions offer, smaller religious movements can form a vital support structure. And for any meditation practitioner, of whatever religious affiliation, small meditation groups can be very instructive and supportive. Group study and meditation can be powerful learning experiences, and it may even be easier for you to find a study group of individual seekers somewhere beyond the doors of the chapel on the corner.

You can find groups that practice meditation through a number of different sources, including weekly newspapers, bulletin boards in supermarkets and laundromats, the Yellow Pages, and, of course, the Internet. Some of these groups are more developed than others. Just because an organization claims to teach meditation or has a large number of followers, don't assume that it is very advanced in its practices and hence capable of lending you helpful instruction. Even if you find a huge, well-established organization, you shouldn't assume a high level of advancement. As in all arenas of life, in the teaching of meditation there are positive and negative teachers; you might find a few nuts, some who are serious but, for all their good intentions, have not developed far enough to be of real help, and, of course, those who are both well developed and balanced. And you may find any of the above in groups of any size.

When you are choosing a group to study with, remember that intuition plays a key role in discerning how far along the journey a particular group is and how much help they can actually be to you. If, for instance, you walk into a situation where you are asked to give all of your worldly possessions to the head "guru," thereby "relieving you of this awful burden," it is likely you would do better somewhere else. Worldly possessions are not a real obstacle to the development of inner peace. As you know by now, the real obstacle is obsession with worldly possessions, or any obsession. Inner peace isn't earned or lost by changing circumstances or behavior. In other words, getting rid of the physical expression won't displace the obsession. It will only make the guru rich.

This is not to say that groups that teach or support meditation don't need money to maintain their community. In our world there is rent to pay, bills are due, and, yes, most people require food to eat — even gurus. Things cost money, and so there is absolutely nothing wrong when any religious or meditation group that offers valuable instruction to its members charges for its services or requests donations. But in my view there is simply no validity in the belief that sacrificing physical possessions brings any sort of advancement. More likely, it causes anxiety and depression, or minimally a sense of deprivation.

Another common clue that foolishness is afoot in a meditation group is when a supposed teacher demands full loyalty and submission from all followers. I think full devotion is due to God, and that respect is every human's fair wage. Personally, I offer respect to anyone walking this Earth with me, in recognition that they are beloved of God, regardless of their behavior. I also offer gratitude to those who share their thoughts and lives with me. I think gratitude and common respect, then, are reasonable gifts to give to everyone. But absolute loyalty and submission are due only to God.

In evaluating a group to work with, then, I recommend that you keep the following points in mind:

- If possible, find out what the group's specific theological views are *before* you contact anyone directly.
- If you are still interested, attend a service or meeting, listen to all that is said regardless of whether you agree with it or not, and delay any evaluation of the group until later, when you are home and can quietly reflect on what you saw and heard.
- Don't make any commitments to come again, even if you think you're just being polite, before you have had enough time to thoroughly appraise the group's views and methods.
- Don't give out your phone number, address, or last name until you feel comfortable doing so.
- Don't offer any major donations at the first meeting.

In your appraisal you should also keep in mind that no group is going to show you all that they are made of when they first meet you, so you need to be able to sense what type of environment the group fosters. Try to sense if the people you meet seem comfortable or ill at ease, and if the leader or leaders seem gracious and welcoming or controlling and arrogant. People who begin to develop a real sense of the power attainable through meditation often use it to wield power over others. This is one of the traps along any spiritual path. Any authentic spiritual teacher, though, should at least have realized that the attempt to control others leads to suffering for both the teacher and the student, and that such control can cause long developmental delays.

In any case, I doubt a seriously advanced being would really desire your own submission and obedience. The fully developed human is one who has transcended human ego and operates from a completely different level. Such a teacher inspires others and lifts them up so that they catch a reflection of their own potential through the teacher. In this there is no force. It is a peace-filled process.

The bottom line is that when dealing with any religious or meditation group, you should use your head first. Observe closely and assess thoughtfully. Then, when you have found a program that suits you and that seems to attract trustworthy people, explore the beliefs freely and develop friendships with others in the group who meditate. When you have finally decided that a place feels right, then you can drop your defenses and put some real heart into your studies. For some people, getting involved with a study group is absolutely the thing they need in order to progress. So don't be timid in your search; just be smart.

retreats

One of the safer ways to explore a group is by attending its retreats. I think everyone who is serious about meditation should do at least one retreat. The United States and many other countries offer a wealth of spiritual communities set aside for just this purpose, and many offer very affordable rates. By setting aside a weekend or even longer for the sole purpose of meditation and contemplation, you can uncork powerful moments and bridge new connections. A sense of commitment and devotion is sometimes only first made real when a devotee attends a retreat and meets with other seekers and advanced teachers. Just the presence of a serious teacher can be enough to inspire you to reach deeper states, and a well-run retreat itself is like a sanctuary from the daily grind.

Retreats can be found through a number of sources. Many can be found on the Internet by using your search engine; simply enter terms like "retreats," "meditation retreats," or "spiritual retreats," or terms more specific to your own religious background, like "spiritual retreats" AND "Catholic" or "spiritual retreats" AND "Hindu." Some of the Websites you will find in this way will be exclusively related to a specific retreat, while others will be directory sites that list links to many retreat sites.

If you don't have access to the Internet, you may want to check with places of worship in your area, the phone book, or with the many spiritually oriented periodicals available at bookstores and libraries. (Listings of retreats are also available in some books, such as *Journey of Awakening: A Meditator's Guidebook,* by Ram Dass, which has both national and state listings.) Or you might check with your favorite spiritual author. Some teachers hold retreats each year in a variety of locations, which are generally rented out for a weekend or so.

As to which sort of retreat you should choose, keep in mind that all retreats are not created equal. The teachings in retreats vary as much as the teachings in places of worship: some retreats are relatively generic, providing meditation practice and teachings that could be helpful to people of many different religious backgrounds, whereas others are specific to one belief system. Additionally, the formats differ: many retreats allow attendees to basically do their own thing while providing a backdrop of teachings you can take or leave as you choose, and others offer guided programs, some of which can be quite rigorous. So be sure to look into the programs *before* you sign up. Ultimately, I think the best retreats, either guided or not, fancy or bare-boned, are those that provide an atmosphere of exploration and discovery, as opposed to dogmatism and control.

With that in mind, you should feel free to explore the belief systems each retreat offers. Learning is advanced in this way. We can't afford to cut ourselves off from varying viewpoints for fear our own beliefs will suffer. Incorporating new ideas into our lives is the root of all growth. Retreats offer forums for the sharing of ideas, providing a place where you can meet and develop important relationships with others and set aside some time exclusively for spiritual development. Attending retreats can be both informative and experiential. Use them like any of the tools we have learned about — to your best advantage.

book learning

Books, such as this one, can also provide much of the instruction, contemplative material, or information needed along any spiritual path, and today there is a larger body of literature available on spiritual and religious topics than ever before. We have access to books on the strangest of topics as well as the most mundane, and plenty of them offer valuable assistance that you can explore safely from your own home. If you are looking for more good books to read, check out the "Recommended Reading" section at the back of this one.

the internal teacher

I've covered a few topics you might encounter as you do some seeking beyond your daily practice, as well you should. But as you experience these guides along the path, there is something you should understand. Each of us carries an internal Teacher, which some call God, others Spirit or Soul. Whatever word you prefer, remember that all paths, religions, groups, retreats, and books are meaningless unless they facilitate contact with this Teacher.

The many forms we use for learning are only useful while we remain fixated on the external world; the spiritual path, however, is internal. We don't really need to seek external guidance. Our Teacher is already within us, and all the many-formed lessons are meant to lead us to this awareness. This is something that is with us wherever we go, whenever we go there, and whatever we do. We don't need to search the world to find an "enlightened teacher." We already have one. Finding our internal Teacher is what all external study should be geared toward, including meditation.

Once you connect with your internal Teacher, learning becomes simpler and self-correcting, leading to internal realizations only experience can demonstrate. In all your studies and doings, remember that although there is no theology in Heaven, we can use our beliefs, our practice, our guides to lead us there. Beyond this end, such tools serve no purpose. Like the heart of meditation, the most helpful theologies teach only the art of letting them go.

epilogue

wherein we hold our course

Our thoughts are the epochs of our lives; all else is but as a journal of the winds that blew while we were here.

— Henry David Thoreau[2]

I n this book I have outlined the beginning steps along a vast and beautiful journey. My message has been simply that life itself is a journey and a gift, which deserves to be embraced and loved. Still, there is much emptiness that needs healing, and so it is that the inner search is vital to bringing our lives to peace — where we can directly experience the joy of the Self, where we feel complete, comforted, and unconditionally loved. In one sense, meditation is an exploration just like those the explorers of old undertook: there is a sense of adventure, uncertainty, and halting discoveries. The difference is that it is an *internal* exploration, one in which a single perfect experience can bring complete understanding of the whole journey. When you experience one perfect instant just as it is, a secret, hidden door suddenly opens, time stops, and the true power of stillness finally awakens.

From here forward I recommend that you continue exploring your life through meditation, twice each day. Over the last month, you have tried many forms. Now it's a good idea to choose the one you felt was the most effective and practice it on a daily basis. As I have already noted, there are subtleties to each kind of exercise that will be revealed only through a deeper commitment.

If, over the long haul, you feel bogged down in dull routines that turn your meditations into uneventful rituals performed out of sheer habit, you can shake things up: Try a different form of meditation, challenge yourself to meditate for longer periods, attend a retreat or workshop, set aside a weekend for extended meditation, prayer, study, silence, or other practices, or simply take some time to pause and mentally recommit yourself to your purpose.

As to how long you should meditate, practicing for fifteen to twenty minutes a day for now is reasonable. After a year or so, most people feel comfortable with thirty-minute sittings. This isn't to say you shouldn't challenge yourself to meditate a little longer than you feel comfortable, but always keep in mind that quality comes before quantity, so you should advance slowly into longer meditations.

After a few years of devoted practice, you might be surprised to find that forty-five minutes, or even a little longer, feels too short.

I cannot overemphasize the importance of continuing your practice of meditation. Meditation is one form of the ultimate path, the highest goal to which a human can aspire. It is a part of the final evolution of humanity from without to within. The deepest experience of meditation is also our resting place — the destination of evolution. The journey is very much the same for all of us. We learn many lessons along the way, yet the ultimate lesson is the recognition that the journey is already finished, that our lives are complete, and that we have no needs exceeding the need to be awakened and to awaken.

Once you have reached this ultimate realization, you will find that the busy world settles down and time winds into a gentle, natural rhythm. The whole world will stop along with you as you celebrate this dawning period of freedom within, and for a moment you will experience a suspension of doubts, of time, of space. You will see your life extend beyond, beyond, and off into a great peace from which the deepest sense of power unfolds.

This silence pervades and touches the lives of all who have come along the path of peace, leaving a gentle blessing in the form of a vision we can use within the confines of our mortal frames, and onward into the mystical heart of Creation. I believe that this is the real power of stillness. It may well be the only power there is. Let us endeavor, together, to uncover the reality of these words through actual experience. This is the heart of meditation. Use it well.

recommended reading

looking for another good read? Here are twelve that enriched my own journey:

- Bach, Richard. *Illusions: The Adventures of a Reluctant Messiah* (New York: Dell Publishing, 1979).

  Considered a classic, this short, fictional book takes the reader on an airplane ride with, as the title suggests, "a reluctant messiah." But there is more to the journey than adventure. Many thought-provoking ideas serve as the central platform around which the story is built.

- Castaneda, Carlos. *The Power of Silence: Further Lessons of Don Juan* (New York: Pocket Books, 1991).

  Castaneda's work has affected millions, giving many their first glimpse into a spiritual thought system beyond the mainstream. In this well-rounded book, many of the insights delivered in the author's previous works finally begin to make sense. It's a fun read, and some say more than that: together with the full body of Castaneda's other works, it describes a complete spiritual path. However one views the book, the words of Don Juan, the central teacher, offer the reader wisdom galore, along with a comical edge unparalleled in metaphysical literature.

- Chopra, Deepak. *The Seven Spiritual Laws of Success* (Novato, Calif.: Amber-Allen and New World Library, 1994).

  Deepak Chopra has been hailed as one of the great thinkers of our age, marrying ageless spiritual wisdom with modern thought and needs and hence making the ancient meaningful to the young. The title of this book sums up the content: Chopra's seven laws are wonderfully, simply outlined. Furthermore, he never shies away from the practical; each law is followed up with a discussion of its application. This is great stuff and will be of tremendous value to those who actually want to apply spiritual wisdom to daily life, as opposed to just chit-chatting about it — something (big surprise) I am all for.

- *A Course in Miracles* (Mill Valley, Calif.: Foundation for Inner Peace, 1996).

  Consisting of over 1,300 pages divided into three main sections — a text, a workbook, and a question-and-answer manual for teachers — this book takes at least a year to work through and is designed to connect students with their internal Teacher. Renowned for its soaring language, which has been compared to some of the most beautiful in literary history, *A Course in Miracles* is an intense program that uses Christian terminology and a psychological foundation to deliver its message. Some students, myself included, believe it to be the most powerful spiritual teaching ever to find its way to Earth. Should you decide to pursue it, beware the initial resistance that most students experience, usually involving rejection of the teaching for one reason or another. Everyone I know who has encountered the work has had a very powerful initial reaction to it, one way or another.

- Dass, Ram. *Journey of Awakening: A Meditator's Guidebook* (New York: Bantam, 1990).

  Ram Dass is well regarded for his honesty and warmth. This book outlines most of what a beginning student of meditation needs to know, and in addition it is thickly laced with some of the most poetic and insightful quotes from teachers of all faiths. As noted above, it also provides a directory to retreats and other groups involved in meditation. For both of these reasons it makes an excellent reference book.

- Dass, Ram. *Miracle of Love: Stories About Neem Karoli Baba* (Santa Fe, N.M.: Hanuman Foundation, 1995).

  A tribute to Ram Dass's guru, Neem Karoli Baba, or Maharajji, *Miracle of Love* is jam-packed with stories about the great Indian spiritual teacher who touched many thousands of followers. Included are some of the most convincing testimonies I have ever read, along with a number of photos that really transport the reader to the time and place of Maharajji's teachings. Somehow, by the time I finished this book, I felt a deep personal connection with this teacher.

- Gibran, Kahil. *The Prophet* (New York: Alfred A. Knopf, 1976).

  Kahil Gibran, who some say was a prophet himself, was a great Islamic poet and philosopher, as is evident in this, his most famous work. The story opens at the point of enlighten ment for the Prophet, who then goes on to address the people's questions before his final earthly departure. The whole is beautifully written and deeply affecting.

- Herrigel, Eugen. *Zen in the Art of Archery* (New York: Vintage Books, 1989).

  One of the first in the long line of *Zen in the Art* books, this one's a classic. Describing his Zen training through archery under the guidance of a Zen master, the author demonstrates the ineffable nature of Zen thinking in the simplest way possible: by making the writing of the book a Zen exercise itself!

- LeShan, Lawrence. *How to Meditate: A Guide to Self-Discovery* (Boston: Little, Brown & Company, 1974).

  This is a simple yet provocative glimpse into the practice of meditation. With over 1 million copies in print, it's had quite a successful run, mostly because it goes where most other books do not. Like most books on meditation, it addresses the methods, but then it goes on to offer some other interesting commentaries on topics such as incorporating meditation into psychotherapy, the paranormal, and the social implications of the practice. It is frank, and while I do not agree with all of the author's views, I did appreciate his candor and spirit. Check it out.

- Williamson, Marianne. *A Return to Love: Reflections on the*

Principles of A Course in Miracles (New York: Harper Collins Publishers, 1992).

Marianne Williamson is the most public figure associated with *A Course in Miracles*. Here she interprets both the "Principles" and the "Practice" of the spiritual path, especially as they pertain to *A Course in Miracles*. The book reflects Williamson's great, infectious enthusiasm for the topic in a comfortable, down-to-earth style. Not just for *A Course in Miracles* students, the book addresses principles that are universal to any spiritual path.

• Yogananda, Paramhansa. *Autobiography of a Yogi* (Los Angeles: Self-Realization Fellowship, 1973).

This book traces the author's life from his days as a child in India to the establishment of Self-Realization Fellowship (SRF), a world-renowned organization that to this day continues to distribute his spiritual teachings. Some of the stories recounted here are incredible — and some readers may think unbelievable — but if the testimony in the back the book is any indicator, they may well be true. One example: After the author's death in 1952, the director of Forest Lawn Memorial Park sent SRF a notarized letter testifying that, to his astonishment, Yogananda's body remained in a "phenomenal state of immutability" for weeks after his death. For further information, browse SRF's Website at: www.yogananda-srf.org.

• Zukav, Gary. *The Seat of the Soul* (New York: Fireside, 1989).

Mr. Zukav won the 1979 American Book Award in Science for his earlier work, *The Dancing Wu Li Masters*. In *The Seat of the Soul* he makes a leap from physics to metaphysics. In a dramatic stylistic shift from the complexity of his first book, this simple book addresses Zukav's belief that humankind is currently undergoing an evolutionary birth into a multisensory level of Life. As the book jacket states, the book "is about this birth, what it means, and how to participate in it wisely."

notes

part 1

1. Saint Basil the Great, Bishop of Caesarea, 4th Century CE, quoted in *Learn to Meditate: A Practical Guide to Self-Discovery and Fulfillment*, by David Fontana (San Francisco: Chronicle Books, 1999), p. 20.
2. Robert H. Schneider, et al., "Lower Lipid Peroxide Levels in Practitioners of the Transcendental Meditation Program," *Psychosomatic Medicine*, vol. 60, no. 1, Jan./Feb. 1998, p. 39.
3. Lawrence R. Murphy, "Stress Management in Work Settings: A Critical Review of the Health Effects," *American Journal of Health Promotion*, vol. 11, no. 2, Nov./Dec. 1996, p. 132.
4. Doriel Hall, *Discover Meditation: A First-Step Handbook to Better Health* (Berkeley, Calif.: Ulysses Press, 1997), p. 6.

part 2

1. Saint Francis, quoted in *Minding the Body, Mending the Mind*, by Joan Borysenko with Larry Rothstein (Boston: Addison-Wesley Publishing, 1987), p. 45.

2. Patricia Monaghan and Eleanor G. Viereck, *Meditation: The Complete Guide* (Novato, Calif.: New World Library, 1999), p. xxiii.

3. *A Course in Miracles: Workbook for Students* (Mill Valley, Calif.: Foundation for Inner Peace, 1996), p. 380.

4. Ibid., Lesson 121, p. 215.

5. Ram Dass, *Journey of Awakening: A Meditator's Guidebook* (New York: Bantam, 1990), p. 6.

6. Kahlil Gibran, *Sand and Foam: A Book of Aphorisms* (New York: Alfred A. Knopf, 1970, 1995), p. 63.

7. Alfred, Lord Tennyson, *In Memoriam* (V), quoted in *The Macmillan Dictionary of Quotations* (Edison, N.J.: Chartwell Books, Inc., 2000), p. 564.

8. Henry David Thoreau, *A Week on the Concord and Merrimack Rivers,* quoted in *Thoreau: On Man and Nature,* compiled by Arthur G. Volkman (Mount Vernon, N.Y.: Peter Pauper Press, Inc., 1960), p. 56.

9. Dan Millman, *Everyday Enlightenment: The Twelve Gateways to Personal Growth* (New York: Warner Books, 1998), p. 69.

10. Neem Karoli Baba, quoted in *Miracle of Love: Stories About Neem Karoli Baba,* by Ram Dass (Santa Fe, N.Mex.: Hanuman Foundation, 1995), p. 183.

11. William Blake, *There is No Natural Religion,* quoted in *The Macmillan Dictionary of Quotations* (Edison, N.J.: Chartwell Books, Inc., 2000), p. 75.

12. Deepak Chopra, *The Seven Spiritual Laws of Success* (Novato, Calif.: Amber-Allen/New World Library, 1994), p. 4.

13. Ram Dass, *Journey of Awakening: A Meditator's Guidebook* (New York: Bantam, 1990), p. 13.

14. Chuang-tse, quoted in *Journey of Awakening: A Meditator's Guidebook,* by Ram Dass (New York: Bantam, 1990), p. 127.

15. Luke 17:20–21 King James Version.

16. Ouida, "Ariadne" from *Wisdom, Wit, and Pathos,* quoted in *The Macmillan Dictionary of Quotations* (Edison, N.J.: Chartwell Books, Inc., 2000), p. 378.

17. Mahmud Shabistari, *The Secret Rose Garden of Shabistari* (Grand Rapids, Mich.: Phanes Press, 1989).

18. Benjamin Jowett, *Autobiography* (Asquith), quoted in *The Macmillan Dictionary of Quotations* (Edison, N.J.: Chartwell Books, Inc., 2000), p. 203.

19. George Herbert, "Discipline," quoted in *Simple Abundance: A Daybook*

of Comfort and Joy, by Sarah Ban Breathnach (New York: Warner Books, 1995), January 26.

20. Matthew 6:22 KJV.

21. Quoted in Derek Prouse, "A Last Talk with Cocteau," *Sunday Times* (London), 20 October 1963, p. 34.

22. Saint Teresa of Avila (1515–82), founder of the Discarded Carmelities, quoted in *How to Meditate: A Guide to Self-Discovery,* by Lawrence LeShan (Boston: Little, Brown, and Company, 1999), p. 78.

23. Eckhart Tolle, *The Power of Now: A Guide to Spiritual Enlightenment* (Novato, Calif.: New World Library, 1999), p. 85.

24. A. A. Milne, *The Complete Tales of Winnie the Pooh* (New York: Dutton Books, 1994), p. 38.

25. Kahlil Gibran, *Sand and Foam: A Book of Aphorisms* (New York: Alfred A. Knopf, 1970, 1995), p. 15.

26. Lawrence LeShan, *How to Meditate: A Guide to Self-Discovery* (Boston: Little, Brown and Company, 1999), p. 14.

27. William Blake, *America: A Prophecy,* quoted in *The Macmillan Dictionary of Quotations* (Edison, N.J.: Chartwell Books, Inc., 2000), p. 73.

28. Scottish proverb, quoted in *The Macmillan Dictionary of Quotations* (Edison, N.J.: Chartwell Books, Inc., 2000), p. 247.

29. Eugen Herrigel, *Zen in the Art of Archery* (New York: Vintage Books, 1989), p. 81.

30. Jean de La Fontaine, "Le Lion et le Rat" (II) from *Fables,* quoted in *The Macmillan Dictionary of Quotations* (Edison, N.J.: Chartwell Books, Inc., 2000), p. 413.

31. Gary Zukav, *The Seat of the Soul* (New York: Fireside, 1989), p. 22.

part 3

1. John Milton, *Areopagitica,* quoted in *The Macmillan Dictionary of Quotations* (Edison, N.J.: Chartwell Books, Inc., 2000), p. 366.

2. Henry David Thoreau, Journal, Vol. 1, No. 5, quoted in *Thoreau: On Man and Nature,* compiled by Arthur G. Volkman (Mount Vernon, N.Y.: Peter Pauper Press, Inc., 1960), p. 29.

about the author

Photo by Lourdes Maria

tobin Blake has studied various metaphysical teachings for more than fifteen years and has been meditating regularly for nearly a decade. Through Self-Realization Fellowship, an international organization founded by Paramhansa Yogananda and now supporting more than 500 temples and meditation centers in fifty-four countries, Blake received training in the sacred practice of Kriya Yoga, the organization's highest meditation technique, which was first noted in Paramhansa Yogananda's classic, *Autobiography of a Yogi.*

In the early 1990s, Blake's life was transformed through his meditation practice when he spontaneously experienced a state he now describes as a "direct revelation of the unity between the Mind of God and humanity." Since then he has dedicated his life to cultivating this mystical awareness within himself, while sharing his insights with others. For the past eight years he has focused his efforts on studying and implementing the principles outlined in *A Course in Miracles,* a teaching that has impacted thousands and altered the course of his own life profoundly.

Blake's short fiction has appeared internationally in *Surfer Magazine* and in *Dead on Demand,* an anthology that spent six months on the *Library Journal* "print on demand" Best-Seller List. *The Power of Stillness* is his first book.

Born and raised in Los Angeles, Tobin now resides in a high-desert community along the eastern flank of the Cascade Mountains in Central Oregon with his wife, Lourdes Maria, and their two daughters, Ashley and Brittany.

For further information visit:
www.tobinblake.com
or
Write Tobin with your comments and questions at:
Tobin Blake
P.O. Box 9007
Bend, OR 97708
E-mail: tobin@tobinblake.com